Thinking about the Baby

Gender and Transitions into Parenthood

IN THE SERIES *Women in the Political Economy,*
edited by Ronnie J. Steinberg

Gender and

THINKING

Transitions

ABOUT

into

THE

Parenthood

BABY

SUSAN WALZER

TEMPLE UNIVERSITY

PRESS

Philadelphia

TEMPLE UNIVERSITY PRESS, PHILADELPHIA 19122

Text design by Gary Gore

Library of Congress Cataloging-in-Publication Data

Walzer, Susan, 1958–
    Thinking about the baby : gender and transitions into parenthood / Susan
Walzer.
      p.   cm. — (Women in the political economy)
    Includes bibliographical references and index.
    ISBN 1-56639-630-1 (alk. paper). — ISBN 1-56639-631-X (pbk. : alk. paper)
    1. Parenthood — Psychological aspects.   2. Parenting — Psychological
aspects.   3. Mother and child.   4. Father and child.   5. Sex role.
I. Title   II. Series.
HQ755.8.W363   1998
306.874 — dc21
                                      97-47742
                                       CIP

Contents

Acknowledgments

Some of the material in this book appeared in a somewhat different form in the articles "Thinking About the Baby: Gender and Divisions of Infant Care," published in 1996 in *Social Problems*, and "Contextualizing the Employment Decisions of New Mothers," published in 1997 in a special issue of *Qualitative Sociology* on families and social policy.

I am very grateful to the parents who agreed to talk with me about their transitions into motherhood and fatherhood. This book wouldn't exist without them, and I appreciate the generosity and thoughtfulness with which they shared their time and experiences.

This book began as a doctoral dissertation guided by Glenna Spitze, Karyn Loscocco, and Jim Zetka. I appreciate all three of them for sharing their talents and wisdom throughout my years as a graduate student at the State University of New York at Albany and beyond. Thank you to Glenna also for encouraging me to find my own voice as a sociologist and for being my friend. Karyn's intelligence and understanding enhance my work and my life.

I am also grateful to all of the members of the Department of Sociology, Anthropology, and Social Work at Skidmore College as well as other colleagues around the college for their support and encouragement. Thank you to Susan Bender, Kate Berheide, John Brueggemann, Gerry Erchak, Bill Fox, and Pat Oles for helpful advice on this project.

Thanks also to Michael Ames at Temple University Press for his editorial insight and to Ronnie Steinberg and other reviewers unknown to me for their constructive readings of previous drafts of this book.

Thank you to my parents, Joyce and Richard Walzer, who got me into the world and have been there for me through thick and thin. My brother, Andy, is the quintessential comrade. My sister, Janet, has performed every function a sister, friend, and editor can perform, and for me defines the term "unconditional love."

Thank you to my friends.

For the things that make sense, thank you to Tim.

I am proud to be the mother of Alex and Leah and dedicate this book to them with love.

Thinking about the Baby

Gender and Transitions into Parenthood

❦

CHAPTER 1

Becoming Mothers and Fathers

ONE OF MY PEAK MOMENTS AS A NEW MOTHER happened during a car ride with my baby. Alex was in front on the passenger side, strapped into his rear-facing infant seat (the advised procedure at the time). I was watching the road very carefully, nervous about having him in the car. When I stopped at a red light and turned to check on him, his eyes were already on me. I was so moved that during the silence of our drive, he had turned his big baby head on his little baby neck to gaze at me.

This book is not about moments like that. It's not about the wonder of holding and touching and smelling and laughing with babies. It's not very much about what happens between babies and parents at all. Rather, this book is primarily about what goes on between women and men who become parents together, and how their negotiations as new parents grow out of their experiences of being women and men in our society. This book is about why, even though mothers and fathers encounter many of the same pleasures with babies, they frequently have very different

1

stresses in becoming parents—differences that strain their relationships with each other.

During a recent discussion with some of my students about the tendency for women in dual-earner marriages to do a disproportionate amount of housework, one person said, "But hasn't that changed? That's not really happening anymore, is it?" As other students talked about what they observed in their own households while growing up, their responses reflected the complexity that has been captured in recent scholarship about family work divisions: that they tap into how we define work and love and masculinity and femininity; and that they are changing and not changing at the same time.

This ambiguity is present in academic interpretations of parenting arrangements as well. While the line between mothering and fathering is beginning to blur (Coltrane 1996), longitudinal studies of transitions into parenthood suggest that they are marked by increases in differentiation by gender (Belsky and Kelly 1994; Cowan and Cowan 1992; Sanchez and Thomson 1997). My students' confusion about what's *really* happening in families was present in my interviews with new parents who, on one hand, spoke as though definitions of mothering and fathering were supposed to have shifted, and on the other hand, couldn't necessarily illustrate that change with their own stories.

I've thought of this book as a way of continuing these conversations and have written visualizing new parents and students as the audience—along with academic colleagues and other people interested in families and gender. There is a sense among the general public and in some scholarly work that motherhood and fatherhood are being redefined, yet there is much old news along with the new. This book is in large part about the old news, which is the power of gender as an organizing feature of the social world.

One new mother that I interviewed, whom I will call Laura, told me about a couple she thought I should talk to because "the dad is like the mom and the mom is like the dad": "She's the one that says, 'Oh I've got to go now,' you know? And he's like, 'When will you be back, dear?'" Implicit in Laura's commentary is the notion that "the mom" is different from "the dad": the dad traditionally goes out into the world while the mom and the baby wait for him. Although this pattern was not literally true for Laura (she and her husband were both teachers), this imagery nevertheless captured Laura's perception of what happens to men and women who become parents together.

In Laura's view, her life had been transformed by motherhood and her "freedom" lost, while her husband Stuart's life had not been affected. She quoted herself as saying to him: "You have no clue what this is like. Your life has not changed one iota." Laura talked about feeling that she had to check with Stuart before making plans that did not include their baby, while Stuart did not check with her first. She described herself asking him, "Can I do this in three weeks?"

Stuart disagreed that his life had been unchanged by the birth of their baby: "I know she doesn't think that it changes as much for the man as it does for the woman . . . but you know, you don't get to go bicycling as much, you don't get to go running. I don't know if I'll play softball this year. I played ball every summer my whole life."

Laura perceived that Stuart's leisure activities still continued, if in reduced form, but hers had not: "He always tells me, 'Oh you could do that, you could do that too. Just tell me when you want to do it.' Well it doesn't fit. Unless I want to do something from midnight to three in the morning."

Stuart didn't buy this: "I've said lots of times, 'Just do it and Nicky and I will be fine.'" He thought that Laura's personal philosophy of baby-raising kept her more physically accountable to the baby than he was, and, Stuart suspected, more than she needed to be: "Sometimes I say, 'He's fine, he's fine,' but he's not fine enough for her." The differences that Stuart and Laura perceived in their lives and identities as new parents as well as the tensions that these perceptions created in their relationship are among the issues that I explore in this book.

I interviewed twenty-five couples about their experiences of becoming parents together to understand more about the polarization between women and men that has been identified in previous empirical studies about transitions into parenthood (see Belsky and Kelly 1994; Cowan and Cowan 1992). According to this research, women and men who create and care for a baby become increasingly unlike one another and differentiated in their work and parenting arrangements, despite their intentions. Women's senses of self merge with caretaking while men find themselves focusing on their "breadwinning" abilities (Cowan and Cowan 1992). Along with these inner changes, women's and men's roles change externally as well, particularly in relation to their divisions of labor (Belsky and Kelly 1994; Cowan and Cowan 1992; Sanchez and Thomson 1997). Men tend to do more paid work after the birth of a baby, while women do less. Women tend to do more domestic work, while men (continue to) do less. These trends toward more stereotypically male and female roles occur regardless of wives' employment status, educational level, and couples' preexisting division of labor or gender attitudes (see studies cited in Belsky, Lang, and Huston 1986 and Sanchez and Thomson 1997).

The division of infant care is often more traditional than either partner expected it to be (Cowan and Cowan 1987). Fathers tend to believe that they should be directly involved with their children, but often they are not (LaRossa 1988). Although today's fathers are more involved in the lives of their infants than their own fathers were, mothers spend more time interacting with babies, planning for them, and taking care of "custodial activities." Fathers tend to act as helpers to the more directly involved, primary parent—the mother (see Belsky and Volling 1987; Berman and Pedersen 1987; Dickie 1987; LaRossa 1986; Thompson and Walker 1989). "The only thing fathers do more frequently than mothers," Belsky and Volling (1987: 59) comment, "is read and watch television."

The changes that new parents experience generate conflict in marriages in a way that does not happen to couples who are not parents (Cowan and Cowan 1992; Crohan 1996). It is not the fact of change that is the problem, but the increased differentiation between women and men (Cowan and Cowan 1992). Women are especially affected by the transition, both in terms of decreases in their marital satisfaction (Cowan and Cowan 1988a; Harriman 1985; Miller and Sollie 1980; Waldron and Routh 1981) and in the level of personal change—both positive and negative—that they experience in the transition to parenthood (Feldman and Nash 1984; Harriman 1983; McKim 1987; Miller and Sollie 1980; Ventura 1987). But there are also indications that some men react to the transition with depression, and men as well as women experience declines in marital quality after having a baby (Cowan and Cowan 1995).[1]

Given that gender differentiation during transitions into parenthood strains many individuals and relationships, why does it happen—even to people committed to avoiding it? This question is answered diversely by the researchers whose longitudinal studies have most recently documented these patterns. While some assert that the tendency for new parenthood to polarize men and women is "natural and normal" (see Belsky and Kelly 1994: 5), others question parents' "innocence" in falling into gendered arrangements, arguing that divisions of baby care represent not necessarily conscious choices made by parents: "It's not just that couples are startled by how the division of labor falls along gender lines, but they describe the change as if it were a mysterious virus they picked up when they were in the hospital having their baby; they don't seem to view their arrangements as *choices* they have made" (Cowan and Cowan 1992: 98).

These commentaries tap into eternal questions about nature and nurture, free will and social structure, that underlie much analysis of human experience and social life. Is our behavior biologically innate or learned in our environment? Do individuals exert control in the social world or are we constrained by it? Returning to our more specific dilemma: Are we programmed to behave in gender-specific ways with babies through evolution or through our individual family experiences, or both? Or are parents free to choose the ways in which they will take care of their babies?

I have posed these questions as if they have yes or no answers, but there are few people who would respond in this way. Even those social scientists who argue for the relevance of biological sex differences in understanding how men and women approach parenthood suggest that different societies will ascribe more or less meaning to these differences. Alice Rossi (1985) suggests in her biosocial approach, for example, that biological and cultural factors interact in determining male and female parenting arrangements. The story that this book tells is about the cultural part of this equation. It is about the role of social processes in new parents' transitions into fatherhood and motherhood (see also Rossi 1968 and LaRossa and LaRossa 1989); and it is about the social construction of differentiation between women and men.

This book is not about how people's individual backgrounds influence their experiences of parenting (although I believe they do). Nor can I resolve the question of whether mothers and fathers bring inherent biological differences to parenting.[2] Whether this is true or not, it does not explain why mothers experience significant stress in entering a role considered to be "natural" for them or why many marriages experience conflict when they function in a division of labor by gender that is also considered to be "natural." A primary goal of this book is to add a sociological piece to this puzzle: to bring the social contexts within which new parents make the transition into parenthood more clearly into view, and to look at parenthood as it intersects with gender.

When I talk here about gender, I am not just talking about a characteristic of individual human beings, but about what Cecilia Ridgeway (1997: 219) describes as a "multilevel system of differences and disadvantages that includes socioeconomic arrangements and widely held cultural beliefs at the macro level, ways of behaving in relation to others at the interactional level, and acquired traits and identities at the individual level." To express this in slightly different words: We associate particular aspects of ourselves with being male or female; this is gender on an individual level. We also express maleness and femaleness through the ways that we relate to each other; this is gender on an interactional level. On a macro or societal level, gender is a property of our social organization and embedded in widely held cultural beliefs (Osmond and Thorne 1993; Ridgeway 1997). These various levels are not independent of each other. For example, people may express their individual beliefs about gender through the way that they interact socially (Deaux and Kite 1987); and these social interactions take place within a larger cultural, structural, and historical context—what I am calling in this book an "institutional" context.[3]

I use the word "institutional" to capture gender as a symbolic construction or system of beliefs (Deaux and Kite 1987; Osmond and Thorne 1993) that both structures and is reproduced in social arrangements such as workplaces, families, and medical institutions. I also use the word "institutional" to differentiate the already existing structural and cultural context in which new parents develop their identities as mothers and fathers from the interactions they have within this context. The production of society is "a skilled accomplishment of its members," as Anthony Giddens (1993: 133) writes, but not "merely under conditions of their own choosing." The Marxian notion that people make their own history, but not just as they please, is relevant to new parents.

"Mother" and "father" are social categories that existed before the individuals I interviewed became parents—or were born. These social categories have particular meanings attached to them—meanings that are socializing influences on new parents and that are institutionalized in cultural imagery associated with motherhood and fatherhood. And institutions, as Peter Berger and Thomas Luckmann (1966: 55) write, "by the very fact of their existence, control human conduct by setting up predefined patterns of conduct, which channel it in one direction as against the many other directions that would theoretically be possible."

What I will suggest in this book is that new parents are channeled toward differentiation by social arrangements, and especially, by cultural imagery that constructs what it means to be a "good" mother or father, wife or husband, woman or man. New parents are strongly guided in particular directions on an institutional level, but because the social order, as Berger and Luckmann (1966: 52) note, is "an on-going human production," new parents also have the possibility to act and to interact in ways that redefine motherhood and fatherhood. Much of that possibility resides in recognizing the ways in which gender differentiation and inequality exist in relationships between women and men. Parenthood unmasks gender; it does not create it.[4]

Gender, marriage, motherhood, and fatherhood are constructed within and between people—we do it. We identify in particular ways, we interact in particular ways, and our society is systematized in particular ways that generate and perpetuate particular forms of difference between men and women. This way of conceptualizing gender is often referred to as the "doing gender" perspective, and it is the primary theoretical framework underlying this book. In this perspective, as Candace West and Don Zimmerman (1987) describe, women and men "do" gender by behaving in ways that "real" women and men, as socially defined, are expected to behave. They also do gender by being accountable to these expectations—even when their behavior veers from typical sex-differentiated behavior: "Doing gender does not always mean living up to normative conceptions of femininity or masculinity; what it means is rendering action *accountable* in these terms" (West and Fenstermaker 1993: 157; see also Coltrane 1996). In this view, doing gender is unavoidable, because differentiating between males and females is embedded in our institutional arrangements, perhaps as much as any other form of social categorization. When we do gender, we respond to divisions between men and women, but we do it in the context of these divisions having already been produced and institutionalized.

In this book, I suggest that "doing parenthood" is a form of doing gender. Many of the parents I interviewed described some version of motherhood and fatherhood as social institutions, an impression that different things are expected of mothers and fathers. Laura's scenario ("I'm leaving" and "When will you be back?") illustrates her sense that motherhood and fatherhood have particular norms attached to them that typically take a certain form in the negotiations of individual women and men. The father is defined, in part, by telling the mother that he's leaving — by being asked by her when he'll be back. The mother is defined by being left — by having to ask when the father will be back. If the mother initiates leaving, according to Laura, she isn't "the mom"; she's "like the dad." If the buck stops with the father — if he has to ask the mother to watch the baby when he wants or needs to leave the house, he isn't "the dad"; he's "like the mom."

Mothers and fathers are defined in interaction — interaction that either supports or changes the institutionalized arrangements and beliefs in which it takes place. It is not a coincidence that women happen to be "the moms" and men are "the dads" most of the time; this is a way that women and men recreate themselves as socially defined women and men. The fact that images of motherhood and fatherhood already exist, and that these social constructions are reinforced on an institutional level through various systems that new parents encounter, constrains the amount of choice that any individual male-female couple has in how they approach becoming parents together. Once an individual performs a role, Berger and Luckmann (1966: 74) note, their conduct "is susceptible to enforcement." The enforcement for women and men to act like "moms" and "dads" lies in economic structures that differentiate work and pay by gender as well as in other social relationships and institutions in which norms for women and men are embedded. In this book I attempt to probe the relationship between motherhood and fatherhood as social institutions and the experiences that individual men and women have in becoming fathers and mothers.

New mothers and fathers negotiate parenthood in a social context full of paradoxes. On one hand, mothers and fathers are supposed to be becoming more alike; and on the other hand — well — they aren't. The scenario that Laura thought was typical — dad goes to work and mom stays home — exists concretely for only a minority of couples. Yet even though the mothers and fathers I interviewed tended to be employed, their divisions of physical and emotional labor did not necessarily parallel the fact that they were both providing financially. In fact, Laura was an employed mother who nevertheless characterized her life as having changed in ways that her husband's had not. The difference was in consciousness as well as in behavior — Laura described herself as feeling more tied to and responsible for their baby. At the same time she suggested that Stuart felt more conscious of being the breadwinner — despite their equal wages.

I don't mean to suggest that new parents simply conform to what they think mothers and fathers are supposed to be. Some of the parents that I met talked about doing what they thought fathers and mothers are "supposed" to do, but those "shoulds" were also part of their own identities. It's just that we don't develop our identities in a social vacuum, and as Martha McMahon (1995: 24) succinctly puts it: "Self is a gendered process." That is, we come to see gender not only as a way in which we are categorized in the world, but as an essential part of ourselves. So while the new parents I interviewed were aware of and reactive to dominant cultural imagery of motherhood and fatherhood, this book will present them as actors in the process of reproducing and rewriting scripts for mothers and fathers.[5] Parenthood is not something that just happens to parents and results in certain outcomes for them (although I know it can feel that way at times). The new parents I spoke to had a sense of social expectations, but they had differing views about what the content of these expectations were, a sense that the imagery was flexible, and diverse ways of responding to this ambiguity.

The analysis in this book is grounded in interview data from fifty new mothers and fathers (twenty-five couples) who were living in upstate New York.[6] Their names have been changed, and some identifying information has been made intentionally vague to protect their confidentiality. I used published birth announcements to locate the couples, all of whom had become parents for the first time together. I sought parents whose babies were approximately one year old because I wanted to talk to people who were still in transition with a first child, but who had established some rhythms and reflections on their experiences. I also wanted to avoid findings related to the postpartum "honeymoon" period (Miller and Sollie 1980), and to control for breast-feeding and the obvious differences in the postpartum physical recoveries of mothers and fathers.[7]

Reaching out to new parents rather than seeking volunteers (the method of most past research about transitions into parenthood) meant that there are couples in my study who would not have gone looking for such an experience. One person asked, for example, whether I was "some weird baby-snatcher," but eventually invited me to her home to meet with her and her husband. Of the couples I contacted, 68 percent of those eligible agreed to participate in an interview. There were other individuals who were interested, but since I wanted to examine the ways in which men and women who share a biological connection to a baby negotiate new parenthood with each other, I did not interview just one member of a couple.[8]

With a couple of exceptions, interviews were conducted in parents' homes at a time they chose (usually evening hours), and wives and husbands were interviewed on the same occasion, first separately and with as much privacy as possible, and then more briefly together upon the completion of their separate interviews. The total duration of these interview sessions ranged from two to four hours. I used a semistructured interview format, covering particular topics (captured now in the chapters of this book) in every interview, but following the flow of the person I was interviewing.

Semi-structured interviews are useful for generating theoretical material because they provide an open and flexible forum for new information to emerge and for the complex ways in which people view their lives to be described. Feminists have argued that particular experiences of women are unknown, in part because they have not been described directly by women (Reinharz 1992). This argument could be made about the parenting experiences of both women and men. Women have had idealized and constricting feelings attributed to them as mothers while men's feelings as fathers have gone largely unrecognized. This methodology invited mothers and fathers to describe their beliefs and feelings without providing any expected responses in the structure of the questioning.

The parents I interviewed ranged in age from twenty-one to forty-four years old (one mother declined to reveal her age), were diverse in paid work experiences and histories, and grew up with varying family structures, religious backgrounds, and economic circumstances. About 40 percent of the new parents I spoke with were raised in poor to working-class households; 60 percent grew up in middle- to upper-middle-class environments. With the exception of one father of partly Hispanic origin, the parents were all white. The children ranged in age from eleven to eighteen months. Fourteen of the children were boys, and eleven were girls. Fifteen of the pregnancies were planned, while ten were not. Twenty-three of the twenty-five couples were married, while two were not.

The lack of racial diversity among the parents I interviewed is an unintentional limitation of my study, and the theoretical implications are unclear. Although there may be differences between African American and mainstream white ideologies related to motherhood (see Collins 1991), some studies of transitions into parenthood with racially diverse samples do not highlight race differences as salient in their findings about gender differentiation in new parents.[9] Susan Crohan's (1996) study of marital quality and conflict in transitions to parenthood suggests that African American and white spouses experience similar kinds of decreases in marital happiness and increases in conflict, although she notes some differences by race in conflict behaviors. Unfortunately, my study cannot shed any light on these issues.

In general, the parents in my study should not be seen as representative of all new parents. Rather, my goal in conducting interviews was to make a grounded theoretical contribution (see Glaser and Strauss 1967) to understanding trends in transitions into parenthood that have been established in larger and more diverse samples of parents.

Another goal of this book is to provide some help to people

undergoing this transition. As I've described, the studies that document increases in gender differentiation also implicate this differentiation in decreases in individual well-being and marital happiness. In a plea for interventions for new parents, and based on their own success in supporting marriages in transition to parenthood, Carolyn and Philip Cowan (1995: 422) go so far as to say: "We believe that as long as it is up to each man and woman to work out a satisfying balance of gender role and work-family issues during the transition to parenthood period, the relationships between them—and between them and their children—will be vulnerable to strain."

I hope in this book to provide new parents with what Charles Lemert (1995: xiii) refers to as "sociological competence": "a capacity to feel, understand, and speak coherently about one's social world." I believe that sociological competence about the interactional and institutional processes that play a role in how people experience new parenthood could ease some of the negative experiences associated with this transition. I hope that it will be helpful to individual women and men to understand that the way that they respond to and arrange themselves around their babies cannot necessarily be separated from their interactions with each other, from the cultural imagery that they carry about what it means to be mothers and fathers, and from the ways that motherhood and fatherhood intersect with the larger project of constructing gender.

Studying the ways in which men and women assign meaning to their transitions into parenthood has implications not only for their satisfaction with their relationships with each other and for their mental health, but for their children as well. The conflicts generated between men and women by new parenthood may have an impact on their parenting, and therefore on their children's developmental outcomes (Cowan and Cowan 1992). Parent-child relationships are not the same across cultures, and the various ways in which they are organized yield differing results for how well children are nurtured. What historical and economic circumstances might determine to be the "correct" model for parenting may not be "right" for children, who may experience less warmth and more hostility from a parent who is too isolated (Bernard 1974).

Studying transitions into parenthood also has implications for understanding how systematic injustice is perpetuated. Parenting arrangements are linked not only to the social construction of gender difference, but to gender inequality as well. When individuals act out gender norms in interaction, as Judith Lorber writes (1994: 6), "they are constructing gendered systems of dominance and power." Drawing on evidence from cross-cultural analysis, Scott Coltrane (1996) argues that parenting and gender inequity are "inalterably" linked; in cultures in which fathers are more involved with child care, men are less misogynistic and women have more social and political power. In this book I suggest that the transition into parenthood is a critical point at which gender inequality is reinforced through negative social and economic consequences of childbearing for women (see Munch et al 1997 and Waldfogel 1997), which are generated in part by the social construction of mothers as essential and fathers as relatively peripheral to babies.

CHAPTER 2

Parental Consciousness and Gender

W HEN I BEGAN INTERVIEWING NEW PARENTS, I was on the lookout for variations; I wanted to understand what made some mothers and fathers more gender-differentiated than others. As my research progressed, however, I was struck more by the similarities than by the differences in the new parents I was meeting. While varying in employment status, gender ideology, and divisions of physical labor, new mothers seemed to be having experiences more like each other than not, and distinct from the transitions of their husbands and partners.

What I realized was that the ways in which new mothers and fathers perceived themselves and interacted with their partners were both more complicated and more simple than dichotomies such as employed/unemployed and involved/uninvolved suggested. What was complicated was that generally individuals did not perceive themselves, nor did their partners, as one thing or another. A father might be relatively uninvolved in caregiving tasks, but both he and his wife perceived him as an involved father. A mother might be working outside the home, but both she and her husband framed her employment as something that did not interfere too much with her primary responsibility: mothering.

That was the complicated part. What was simple was that, with some exceptions that I will describe as we go along, there did seem to be one basic dichotomy: mothers and fathers. New mothers were having a different experience than new fathers were, and their interactions with each other appeared to acknowledge and sustain this difference. In some cases the difference was reflected in divisions of caregiving and economic arrangements, but in more cases, it was manifested in nonbehavioral ways. I do not mean to imply here that if you've seen one mother or father you've seen them all. There have been class differences noted among mothers, for example, but these same researchers also point out that there is an overriding similarity in women's approaches to mothering (Hays 1996; McMahon 1995).

Gender differentiation is reflected not only in the concrete divisions of labor of new parents, but in their thoughts and feelings about their babies—what I refer to as their "parental consciousness." I use "consciousness" in two senses of the word. Consciousness refers to mindfulness or awareness, so when I talk about parental consciousness, I am talking about how babies fill parents' minds. I also use it to underscore that the internal experiences that new mothers and fathers report are, in part, a social product—born out of interaction and shaping their actions (Ritzer 1983). In other words, parents think about their babies, and they also think about these thoughts; they judge these thoughts by how they think they *should* be thinking about their babies.

The process I am referring to is captured in George Herbert Mead's concept of the self as both subject and object. In Mead's view, the self arises out of social experience; we experience our selves by observing ourselves as others see us. New parents' identities emerge in a social process: they observe others' responses to them as mothers and fathers, and this observation shapes their identities as mothers and fathers. Bill illustrates this in talking about what happens when he is out in the world with his daughter: "When I'm with her, people call me sir. I don't know, I look at myself in the mirror and picture myself as seventeen, but I have a lot more responsibilities. I'm not as carefree as I was before." When people call Bill "sir," he thinks about how he views himself. On one hand, he does not see himself as others do, and yet he goes on to claim in himself the characteristics that make him a "sir," a father: he has responsibilities and is less carefree than he was before his daughter was born.

In "doing gender" terms, the parents I interviewed carried particular images of what mothers and fathers were supposed to think about—what their responsibilities and feelings were supposed to be—and they were accountable to these images. The process of claiming the socially defined characteristics of a mother or father was not necessarily always conscious, but there were parents who described thinking that they should be worried about something that they weren't in fact worried about, or thinking that they should be feeling something different from what they were actually feeling. Parents also actually had the thoughts and feelings that they thought mothers and fathers should have, as Bill did, and in the group of parents that I interviewed, mothers tended to have different parental consciousness than fathers did.[1] These differences seemed to emerge, in part, out of the experience of caring for the baby, but they also emerged in the context of other social processes. And they played a role in reproducing gendered divisions of baby care.[2] The following narrative about Brendan and Eileen illustrates these points.

BRENDAN AND EILEEN: THINKING LIKE A FATHER AND A MOTHER

Brendan and Eileen both grew up in white, nuclear, middle-class families. They were among the older parents that I interviewed and had well-established careers prior to becoming the parents of their son, Jimmy. Brendan's work in the medical field and Eileen's career as a manager earned them salaries of more than seventy-five thousand dollars each. Eileen described herself as someone who didn't expect to have children. She said that her career was her priority until she met Brendan and subsequently gave birth to Jimmy. Although Brendan and Eileen both expressed deep love for Jimmy, Eileen had many more questions about her mothering than Brendan did about his fathering. This internal form of differentiation reinforced differences in their behavior with Jimmy.

Both Eileen and Brendan characterized Jimmy as a strong connecting force in their marriage. This was not a couple whose relationship had been strained by becoming parents together; rather, Brendan characterized Jimmy as the "glue" in a marriage of "two very different people." Eileen agreed that Jimmy was a bond: "I can think Brendan is an absolute dope and then I'll see him outside with Jimmy and all of a sudden he's wonderful again."

When Eileen talked about Jimmy, she referred to him as a kind of masterpiece, using the language of someone identified with producing and accomplishing things: "I like to think that I've accomplished a lot professionally and personally, but he's far and away the greatest thing I've ever had anything to do with." Brendan also talked about Jimmy as "probably the best thing we ever did," saying he was "perfect in every way, shape, and form."

Brendan said that he likes being in medicine, although he sometimes would rather be doing something else other than going to work. He appreciated that his pay is good and that he works in a setting that is relatively flexible for the demands of his profession. Eileen identified strongly with her career; early in my interview with her, she mentioned opportunities for development and promotion that were being presented to her and that she was currently turning down. After describing the irony that Brendan has a career more easy to move in and out of than her own, she said, "So we both have pretty much decided that we'll scale back on mine and try and kind of hold the line on his." When I asked how that decision was made, she replied, "That's a good question. I don't know if it was a conscious thing."

In many couples, the ways in which they differentiated by gender was not "a conscious thing," but simply something they did. In this case, however, Eileen was aware of connections between her commitment to her paid work and how she approached being a mother. On one hand, she described Jimmy as having enhanced and put her job in perspective: "I'm a lot more creative. I'm more willing to do things that if I was really focused on being promoted by the end of the year, I wouldn't take some of the risks I've taken." I asked her what she saw as the connection, and she explained, "I really think that right now I have discovered that there's something more important. And I've also discovered that if [employer] goes away, it's okay, because I think that I have in some sense found enough confidence in myself that I could go out and find another job."

On the other hand, despite Eileen's greater confidence at work, her love of her job made her feel less confident about herself as a mother, and she attributed a lot of her behavior and feelings to her not being home with Jimmy full-time. Eileen described asking herself: "Why did I have a child if I wasn't going to spend a lot of time with him?" She and Brendan had frequent discussions about how she could work part-time, a solution she felt the need to defend: "Because I think work's an important part of my equation. I just think I get a lot of psychic stuff out of it so I don't think not working is an option for me."

The fact that Eileen traveled for her work meant that there were times that Brendan functioned as Jimmy's primary caregiver. But when Eileen was home, she wanted to do it: "I think Brendan would tell you I do most of the baby stuff, but Brendan's pretty, Brendan's really involved. I mean if I have to [travel for work], he just moves in as primary caregiver." I asked what she meant by "baby stuff": "Like the clothes, the diapers, and I get up in the middle of the night. And I usually put him to bed and that kind of thing. And it doesn't take anything away from Brendan because those are things I want to do."

As a result of her sense of not being as available to Jimmy as she thought she should be, Eileen wanted to do everything she could for him when she was with him. When I clarified that Eileen was saying that she does most of the caregiving when she's home because she wants to, she added that she also thinks it's "the traditional role," and she wondered if she would feel differently about being the primary caregiver if she were home: "If I were responsible for child care twenty-four hours a day, would I be as cheerful as I am about getting up at three in the morning? I don't know, you know?"

I asked if it was in conjunction with her work life that she wanted it this way, and Eileen agreed, "Oh yeah. I mean, maybe it's my way of getting more time or having a bigger role in Jimmy's life, is what I suspect it is." She referred to her behavior with Jimmy as her "stake" in his life: "This is going to be hard to say. It's really important to me that Jimmy understands I'm his mother, whatever that means, because I'm probably not a traditional mother by any stretch."

Brendan characterized their division of labor as something they "fell into": "Well first of all, the first three months when I came home, I mean, she was very possessive, she was fairly possessive and insecure . . . But the other thing is she had breasts and I don't. So we were breast-feeding and it's pretty simple, you know? You breast-feed, and she got a lot of joy out of doing all that stuff—the bumpers, the little bed, the diapers, everything this way and that way—that was fine."

Brendan's comments illustrate the difficulty the new parents I met frequently had in identifying why they do things as they do. In Brendan's case, he attributed their division of labor to Eileen's insecurity and breasts, although the connection between these characteristics and Eileen's enjoyment of setting up the crib, the diapers, "everything this way and that way" was not evident. As I pursued with Brendan his understanding of the role breast-feeding had played in establishing each of their relationships to Jimmy, he identified a difference in the degree of importance that taking care of Jimmy held for Eileen and for him. When I asked him if he would have gotten up in the night to feed Jimmy with a bottle, he laughed, "Not if she wanted to."

"So it was sort of the breast-feeding and then something else?" I asked.

"I'm very happy to let her do it . . . because it's not a big issue for me," he said.

For Eileen, it was a big issue that Jimmy "know" that she is his mother. This appeared to be the source of what Brendan identified as her insecurity and possessiveness; she had to be preferred by Jimmy to everyone else. I asked her to clarify what she meant by wanting Jimmy to know that she was his mother. She explained, "It means that if I come home some night and he's with [his] day care [provider] and he doesn't want to leave her, it'll kill me, is what it means. So I don't know if the rest of this is trying to ensure that doesn't happen. I don't know if the rest of it is trying to ensure that I have that very special role with him." Eileen saw her "special role" with Jimmy as more fragile because of her employment—it was something that she had to work to preserve: "You know it would be something if I were home all day, he would prefer me, is probably a logical train of thought from that, right?"

She said that it had bothered her recently when Jimmy had shown a preference for Brendan over her. She talked to Brendan about this and reported that he was not bothered by Jimmy's usual tendency to show a preference for her.

Brendan recognized Eileen's feelings as emerging out of her desire to be "a good mother," which he described as both "something that she likes" and "from guilt." He suggested that his own behavior with Jimmy was not driven by guilt as Eileen's was: "Well I think she feels that need, she wants to be a good mother. It's something that she likes to do, to be a good mother. From guilt to be a good mother. You know like she feels like, sometimes she'll say, somebody else has raised our son." I asked if he wanted to be a good father, and he replied, "Oh yeah."

"But you don't feel guilty about anything you're doing in relation to that?" I asked.

"No."

Brendan contrasted his "just being a father" with Eileen's approach to being "a good mother." He said that his actions were not dictated by worry about being a bad father and implied that his wife's were shaped by her concern with being a good mother: "I don't operate on guilt, I don't know what guilt is. If there's a way I want to be with Jimmy then I want to do it, or if he's happy I'm happy. We'll work it out together. It's just being a father. It's not a guilt thing. It's not like I'm going to do this because I don't want to be a bad daddy. That's not the case. I do it because I'm having fun doing this."

Eileen believed that her tendency to worry made her less of a good mother in Brendan's eyes: "I think his issue with me as a mother is that I worry a lot." But then she continued, "The fact is that I do, but I also think mothers worry a lot."

On the surface, Eileen and Brendan had less gender differentiation than many couples. They both continued to do paid work. They both participated in the care of their child. Yet it is clear from this narrative that their internal lives — their consciousness of their parenthood and its impact on them — were quite different. Although many of the fathers and mothers that I interviewed expressed a sense of experiencing a new place in the social world, mothers tended to sound like other mothers and fathers like other fathers in describing these changes.

INDIVIDUAL CHANGES

Several of the women that I interviewed reported feeling a particular kind of social acceptance upon becoming mothers. The metaphor used was of having become part of a "club" that conferred on them a new status with other women, as Laura described: "I feel like I've joined a whole new dimension of other people. I wasn't in that club before. And we have this person that I have a lot of respect for that I work with and . . . she came up to me, she put her arm around me, and she said, 'You're about to venture into something that you've never experienced before in your entire life.' She said, 'You're about to become a member of this very unique club.' And I was like Wow! That's cool!" New fathers also felt a commonality with other parents, but they did not tend to focus on being accepted. Rather, they described themselves having a new acceptance of other people's behavior:

> *I've always seen other people with kids and I've always been real bored with them doting over their kids and all the little hurdles and landmarks they reach, but when you have your own kid, it really is different. (Peter)*

> *I guess you become more forgiving of other adults. You never knew why they were so wacky and it's because they have kids. (Tom)*

The ways in which new mothers and fathers talked about losing time, as well as their experiences of their babies' dependence, resulted in different internal responses to the loss of autonomy and mobility that caring for a baby generates.

Virtually all of the parents I interviewed remarked on the change that having a baby made in the amount of time they had for themselves and their partners. Constance said of her son, "My time is his." Even a father who declined to participate in my study said on the telephone, "Maybe you could put that in your paper — there's no time." Yet the stresses that the mothers and fathers I spoke with experienced in relation to time tended to be different. To summarize simply, many mothers experienced stress about time they *didn't* spend with their children, while many fathers were stressed by time they *did* spend with their children in relation to other things they were not getting done. I do not mean to imply that mothers wanted to spend all of their time with their babies or that fathers did not, but that they felt a different accountability about their time, which came through in how they talked about this issue.

Fathers were more apt to address the time that a child requires in negative terms. Phil remarked, "It's almost like you're held hostage to the kid," and Chad said, "I wish I could enjoy it more. For whatever reason at times I can't. And maybe when he gets older and can talk and all that then we will have it easier but right now it's like a one-way street and you got to take care of him. That's just the nature of things."

While it is probable that some mothers shared these sentiments, they did not express them as openly as fathers, who expressed discomfort with the lack of productivity they experienced while spending time with their child:

> *I mean if I'm watching him during the day—she's at work—forget about doing anything. It's constant attention. You can't read, you can't study, you can't paint, you can't do anything. You really got to sit there and watch him. (Peter)*

> *Sitting two hours playing with him, when I first did it was like, this is a waste of my time. I said, "I have more important things to do." And I'm still thinking, "Look at the time I've spent with him. What would I have done otherwise?" (Chad)*

One father, Jack, talked about having difficulty connecting with his baby during the first month. When I asked whether he thought there was something about the baby's behavior, he responded, "Yeah, the fact that he keeps laying there and not doing anything." Jack referred to his feelings as normal, but it is unlikely that a mother who did not feel a connection to her baby for a month would consider her response normal. In fact, for many women, the onset of postpartum depression is signaled by guilt brought on by the fact that they do not feel about their newborn babies what they expect to feel (Taylor 1996).

Phil admitted that at times he thought it might have been a mistake to have a child.[3] Unlike Jack, he did not think that his response was normal and described himself as feeling closed in: "Kind of like my life was never going to be the same. Kind of like spring came around, normally do more stuff outside, away from home. It kind of dawned on me that things weren't getting any less demanding dealing with Louise. Things that I would normally do, go out and play tennis or go to the driving range, hit some balls, it just wasn't working out."

Phil's despair about losing certain leisure activities was in contrast to what one mother, Ruth, described as how she deals with her "working mom's syndrome": "I find if I can be home at five, I can have five to eight, but if I stop at the gym and work out, I'm not home till 6:30. I only have an hour with him. So I've pretty much given up that." Another mother, Liza, talked about making the "obvious" choice to give up contact with her friends: "I used to on my days off always go out with my friends and stuff and I don't do that, obviously, now, and it's great. I just love being here with him."

For mothers, the question was not what else they could be doing with their time, but whether they were giving their children enough time:

> There are still times when I'm like, am I not spending enough time with her? But I spend all my time with her. (Melissa)

> Sometimes I feel a little guilty that . . . I have a little bit more that I should be giving him. (Peggy)

> I just think it is very hard both working full-time and trying to keep the important part of family to me, you know, spending time with her. (Harriet)

In contrast to Harriet's notion that the important part of family is spending time with her daughter, some fathers felt that the time they spent with their children was unimportant relative to other things they had to do. Mothers were less apt to allow themselves to prioritize anything beyond the time they had to spend in their workplaces as important enough to trade off for time with their children. These reactions may be related to the different ways in which the men and women that I interviewed responded to their children's dependence on them.

Many of the mothers and fathers that I spoke with described a new consciousness that evolved with having a baby: a sense that there was someone relying on them. The ways that they talked about this dependence, however, often reflected a gendered dichotomy between financial and other kinds of care. One father, Brett, who described himself as preoccupied with financial matters, joked that the meaning of becoming a father for him was "one more deduction" on his taxes. Other fathers were more sober in describing their concern with providing and planning for the future:

> *It's more pressure. You want better things for your baby so you apply more pressure to yourself. . . . Pressure to succeed so that you can give your family and your children more than what you perceived as what you had. (Jake)*

> *I'm concerned a lot more with the future. I mean, before we had plans, but now you've got to take into account saving money for college. (Gil)*

> *I think about everything a little bit differently. . . . Everything from simply when to take a vacation day, and now you think about, what would [child] like to do? Should we take that trip next year because he'll be old enough to enjoy it? Just everything in general. Financially you start thinking about have you been doing the wisest thing with your funds with the price of college and all going up. (Ted)*

Financial responsibility was perceived by some of the men I interviewed as a unique way in which babies need their fathers. One father, Jay, talked about other caregiving as something he did if his wife was not available; economic provision was something that his baby needed particularly from him: "Someone needs me. I mean Dylan depends on me, you know? Whether it is feeding him or changing his diapers and playing with him when Gloria is not here or whatever. Or just the financial aspect to work, cause I mean if something happened to me, Gloria would just carry on,

I mean she could survive and stuff. But Dylan, you know, he couldn't."

Sometimes this sense of financial responsibility was reinforced by wives who had left jobs or were working part-time:

> *Jay is going to be job hunting and stuff and that really consumes him right now. Of course he is worried, you know, he's the breadwinner in the family, so I think it kind of scares him. (Gloria)*

> *I think it scares him a lot more than he will let on . . . because he knows that he has to take care of her. I could get a job and I could take care of myself, but he has to take care of her. (Whitney)*

> *I think he now feels differently, like he has to take care of his family and he has to be the breadwinner or whatever. Even though we probably make just as much money, you know, our salaries are compatible. But I just feel that he has that different dimension. (Laura)*

Fathers did not tend to question the need to go to work, nor did they see their work demands as affecting their identities as good parents, as Eileen did. Some experienced loss in relation to time they could not spend with their babies when they were at work, but they described their babies' abilities to make them forget their work days when they came home, and there was pleasure in their descriptions of going to work and then coming home:

> *I go to work, I come home, and I feel so refreshed when I'm around him. (Todd)*

> *You can always come home and you can be guaranteed that he'll be there smiling. It helps you forget about your job. It puts things in perspective; it's just a job. (Chip)*

It's nice coming home and having a bad day at work and see-
ing Dylan and he'll come running up with his arms up, you
know, and it just makes all your worries just melt away. (Jay)

For Bill, the tensions around employment and parenthood
came up in his ambivalence about doing jobs besides his primary job:

I do that for extra money to make sure that we do have things
but then I think as I'm doing it, I'm not home with her. I'll get
home, I'll be home for a half hour, and she'll go to bed . . . In
one respect I want to have the money. In another respect, is
that going to make me all that happy? Having maybe a little
bit extra but missing out on, I think I've missed out on, I've
been there for everything, but I haven't been there right on the
spot. Like the first time she really walked. I mean like I came
home, I was there, but I wasn't right there. I don't want to miss
out on that stuff.

Fathers like Bill experienced their absence from their babies
as a loss for themselves while mothers expressed concern that
their absence would result in loss for their babies (and perhaps
more unconsciously, for their sense of themselves as mothers). It
is clear that these fathers felt a sense of responsibility in relation
to their babies. As Elliot said, "I've become somebody's father figure, somebody's role model." Yet as much responsibility as fathers
felt to support their children financially and otherwise, the mothers I interviewed tended to describe a more minute-to-minute,
pervasive sense of ultimate responsibility, as Mandy illustrated:
"The minute they're born you just become this protective thing
that takes care of this baby. You become less of yourself and more
of something that's there for the baby."

The experience that Mandy describes of becoming less of herself is one that has been identified in other research about parenthood. Motherhood appears to take up more of women's identities than fatherhood does of men's. All invest in parenthood, but

fathers tend to hold onto other parts of themselves more than mothers do (Cowan and Cowan 1992).

Motherhood is a state of "being" while fatherhood is something that men "do," according to Diane Ehrensaft (1990: 98), who argues that it is harder for mothers to create boundaries between themselves and their children than it is for fathers: "Mothers are connected while fathers are separate." This sense of connection, McMahon (1995: 268) notes, is one of the greatest rewards of being a mother for the women that she interviewed, but its flip side — feeling responsible — is the worst thing about being a mother. And it is this sense of ultimate responsibility for children that the women McMahon spoke with perceived as one of the great differences between mothers and fathers.

This difference appeared between the mothers and fathers that I interviewed as well. It is not that fathers did not feel responsibility for their babies, but it tended to take a different form than the ultimate responsibility that mothers described. This, McMahon reports, is the biggest downside of being a mother, and many of the women I interviewed also presented this as a source of stress.

I did not attempt in my study to measure men's and women's levels of satisfaction and stress, but there were few clear differences apparent in the positive feelings that the men and women I interviewed reported about having a baby. While it has been suggested that fathers are slower to develop attachments to their babies than mothers are (Belsky and Kelly 1994), I spoke to parents whose babies were about one year old, a time by which most of the women *and* the men were very attached.

But how people feel about their babies is a separate issue from what happens to women and men who become parents together. As we explore differences by gender in parents' sense of responsibility for children, we can begin to see why many new parents, and mothers in particular, do not experience these differences as good news. At the same time, even though these differences exist, they have varying degrees of consequence for the amount of stress and conflict that individuals and couples experience. Mandy, for example, was a mother who was challenged but did not express negative feelings about her sense of responsibility for her baby:

> *This is probably the toughest thing that I have ever done. It's all the time and the minute you have the baby you just real- ize you would do anything, you would go to any extreme to make this baby happy, and you don't put any limits on your- self. You don't say, "I'm going to work on this until 2:00 and if it doesn't work then forget it." You are just constantly work- ing at it and trying to make that baby happy. And I think by the end of the day when that baby finally goes to sleep you think, "This is harder than any eight-hour job I've ever had."*

In contrast to the fathers who perceived their children as pleasurably different from their jobs, Mandy described mother- hood as a job in itself and one that is harder than other work (see also Hays 1996). It is striking that Mandy did not talk about the job of motherhood in terms of concrete tasks. Rather, the job is "trying to make that baby happy." Laura also talked about making her baby happy as part of her job description as a mother. Her baby had a period of crying for four hours in the evening every single night that she *did* describe as stressful "because you think that you're supposed to remedy that; that's your job."

Mandy had returned to an upwardly mobile position in her place of employment after her son was born, then quit her job to stay at home when a family member could no longer look after him. This kind of employment behavior was a clear source of gender differentiation, reflecting how much more directly re- sponsible mothers felt for their babies than fathers. New mothers tend to make more career sacrifices than fathers do, leaving or curtailing employment (Belsky and Kelly 1994).

Laura and Stuart capture this pattern. Laura described changes she had made in her primary teaching job while Stuart was hav- ing trouble adjusting his expectations for himself in extracurric- ular work above and beyond his teaching. Stuart said of his second- ary activities: "I either want to be involved to do it the right way or I almost don't want to be involved at all. Because I don't want to do a less than good job."

Laura was also very identified with her work, but described having to cut out pieces of her job: "I always stayed late at work . . . I always would do work at home. I would always go to the mall and think about what [was] needed at [workplace]. I spent time with parents, meetings, all that kind of stuff, and I can't do that anymore. None of that stuff."

Laura's sense that she simply could not do parts of her job anymore had to do with not wanting her son to be with a baby-sitter for too many hours of the day: "I can't do that, I can't emotionally. I probably could—we'd have to pay more money for the sitter, but I don't want him at the sitter like for ten hours a day. To me, that's, I'm doing something that I want to do, but in the long run, I'm hurting him, you know? In my mind I think that."

What went on in Laura's mind about the consequences of her being away from her son did not go on in Stuart's mind. Other mothers, however, described similar anxiety as well as a more general sense of relentless responsibility and expectation (see also Hays 1996). Laura said: "I want everything to be perfect and you just, you can't. I just have to tell myself that everyday." The image of running at full capacity, and full capacity not being enough, was a feature of women's parental consciousness rather than a response to any particular task per se:

> I don't walk around like a time bomb ready to explode, I don't want you to think that. It's just that I've got this stuff in the back of my head all the time. (Miranda)

> You're trying to be all things to all people and you just can't. (Beth)

Sylvia, who had a successful career, described herself as never before having felt the way she now does as a mother: "I wish I had more confidence in myself. I give this baby so much love. I wish I felt more confident about what I was doing. I just wish that I could trust in what my decisions are and go with that, and I'm trying." In attempting to explain why she feels so insecure, she said, "I have the responsibility for this little guy's whole life and I feel that parents so influence how a kid turns out and sometimes it's like I don't know what the hell I'm doing. I mean, I don't know how I'm going to get this kid to sleep later and I don't know how I'm going to get this kid to play on his own."

While mothers felt more ultimately responsible for babies than fathers, differences in parental consciousness between men and women were also reinforced by their divisions of the care of their babies, of which women tended to do a disproportionate amount (see also Belsky and Volling 1987; Berman and Pedersen 1987; Dickie 1987; Thompson and Walker 1989).

DIVISIONS OF BABY CARE

Approximately one-third of the mothers and fathers that I interviewed reported having a relatively equal division of labor, while two-thirds did not. In this discussion of baby care, I want to emphasize the interactional climate in which women's additional caregiving takes place, as well as forms of more "invisible" or mental labor (see DeVault 1991). I discuss three categories of mental labor involved in taking care of a baby—worrying, processing information, and managing the division of labor—and I suggest that even in cases in which fathers are participating in physical care, mothers tend to be in charge of mental labor. This is consistent with Jay Belsky's finding that even dedicated fathers rarely assume managerial chores such as scheduling doctor's appointments or knowing when it is time to buy new diapers (Belsky and Kelly 1994). I suggest, however, that the difference in men's and women's participation in mental baby care goes beyond remembering to do things; it is both an outcome of, and a sustaining force in, gender-differentiated parental consciousness.

My use of the term "mental labor" is meant to differentiate this less visible work from physical tasks—to capture the internal and interpersonal work that is part of infant care. I include in this category what has been called "emotion," "thought," and "invisible" work in other sociological analyses (see Hochschild 1983; DeVault 1991); that is, I identify aspects of baby care that involve thinking or feeling, managing thoughts or feelings, and that are not necessarily identified as work by the person doing it.

Worrying

> *My mind is always on something, you know, how is he? Or how's he eating? Or how he's this or that, how he's doing in day care.* (Sylvia)

> *I worry about her getting cavities in teeth that are not even gonna be there for her whole life. Everything is so important to me now. I worry about everything.* (Miranda)

> *It's like now you have this person and you're always responsible for them, the baby. You can have a sitter and go out, yes, and have a break, but in the back of your mind, you're still responsible for that person. You're always thinking about that person.* (Peggy)

Regardless of their employment status, the mothers that I interviewed tended to worry (see also Ehrensaft 1990; Hays 1996). Eileen described thinking about their babies as something that mothers do: "Mothers worry a lot." Worrying was such an expected part of mothering that the absence of it might challenge one's definition as a good mother. Alison said of her first day back at her job after being home with her baby: "I went to work and I basically had to remind myself to call and check on him once, I felt, or I'd be a bad mother."

This is a good example of "doing gender" accountability. Alison wasn't actually worried about her baby, but she felt that she had to behave as though she was or she would be a bad mother. Fathers do not necessarily think about their children while they are at work, nor do they worry that not thinking about their child reflects on them as parents (Ehrensaft 1990).[4]

The tendency for mothers to think and worry about babies appeared to be an important source of differentiation within the couples I interviewed, and it presented a paradox for women. On one hand, worrying was associated with irrationality and unnecessary anxiety, and some fathers suggested that their partners worried too much about their babies. As Stuart said of Laura: "Sometimes I say 'He's fine, he's fine,' but he's not fine enough for her." On the other hand, worrying was perceived as something that good mothers do. A number of fathers made an explicit connection between good mothering and their wives' mental vigilance:

She's a very good mother. She worries a lot. (Peter)

She's always concerned about how she's doing or she's always worried about if Carrie's feelings are hurt or did she say something wrong to her. (Gil)

Why is worrying associated with being a mother? I suggest two general reasons, which generate two kinds of worry. The first is that worrying is an integral part of taking care of a baby. It evokes, for example, the scheduling of medical appointments, babyproofing, or a change in the baby's diet. What I refer to as *baby worry* is generated by the question: What does the baby need? And babies need a lot.[5] Baby worry is usually performed by mothers because they tend to be the primary caregivers; however, it can also be carried by fathers in cases in which they take primary responsibility for their babies.

The two fathers that I met who spent more time with their babies than their wives also experienced worry more typical of mothers. One of these fathers, Tom, described a subsuming of himself into the care of his child similar to what some mothers described: "If I'm going to be Hannah's dad, I have trouble with watching her all day and then going to work and trying to see who I am at the same time. So I don't think I'm doing much personal development, learning skills or anything like that. Until she gets old enough that I don't have to watch her all the time."

Other research also suggests that there is a connection between taking responsibility for physical care and baby worry (see Coltrane 1989, 1996; DeVault 1991). It may be, as Sara Ruddick (1983) suggests, that behaving like a mother makes one think like a mother. And although I have only two men as examples, I will speculate that not behaving like a father makes one not think like a father. What I mean is that the two fathers in my sample who spent more time with their babies than their wives did were men who were not particularly identified with their employment; their parental consciousness did not revolve around their planning for the future and being breadwinners.

Arnie described himself as having a checkered work history and was openly ambivalent about a job that he had switched to because the hours were better for his family (a move more typical of mothers). He described guilt about his daughter spending time with a baby-sitter in a way that was also more typical of mothers: "Well I'll tell you that's like ninety nine and nine tenths of the battle to be able to go to work and know she's not going to be propped with a bottle, and even still we got the best of the best with the sitter and it still affects you."

I asked him how it affects him, and he replied, "How in just that you want to know what's going on for your daughter and you want the best for her and you just want a good environment and I don't think there is any place in the world that I could have more comfort, but you still wonder and you still care and you want to know what's going on and you feel guilty."

This leads to the second reason that new mothers tend to worry, which is that social norms make it particularly difficult for mothers to feel that they are doing the right thing. I call this *mother worry*, and it is generated by the question: Am I being a good mother? While there may be psychological explanations for the tendency for mothers to worry, and in shared parenting families, for mothers to worry differently from fathers (see Ehrensaft 1990), what I want to emphasize here is that mother worry is induced by external mechanisms as well. That is, mothers feel connected to their children and see their children as extensions of themselves in a way that prompts worry (Ehrensaft 1990); mothers are also aware that their children are perceived by others as reflecting on them. Some of the mothers that I interviewed expressed worry about how others evaluated them as mothers:

> *I think that people don't look at you and say, "oh there's a good mother," but they will look at people and say, "oh there's a bad mother." (Sarah)*

> *Being a mother I worry about what everyone else is going to think. (Maggie)*

Perhaps Maggie worried about what people thought of her as a mother because she shared the view that mothers are ultimately responsible for children: "The behavior of the child reflects the mother's parenting . . . I mean kids, you have all these things with kids shooting people, and I blame it on . . . mothers not being around."

Baby worry and mother worry are different though related forms of worry. It is evident how baby worry can be characterized as mental labor; it is an integral part of the more obvious physical tasks involved in taking care of a baby. Worrying that a baby is cold, for example, leads to clothing the baby warmly. While the productiveness of mother worry may be less apparent, it is connected to mental labor. Worry about whether one is being a good mother reinforces mothers enacting baby worry as well as other forms of mental labor such as seeking information about baby development and illness.

Worrying is therefore not only induced by mothers' desires to be perceived as taking care of their babies correctly, it is also part of how they *do* take care of their babies. Miranda described her "stressing out" as linked to her getting things done on time; Gil's job was to tell her to lighten up: "I'm the one who stresses out more. He is very laid back. He doesn't worry about things. In fact he procrastinates. And I'm the one, run run run run run. . . . But one of us has to get things done on time and the other one has to keep the other one from totally losing it and make them be more relaxed. So it kind of balances us out."

Liza said of her interactions with Peter: "He'll say, 'Whoa it's time to go to bed' and I'll say, 'Well Peter, you know, I've got to make bottles. I've been working all day and you think they're just going to get done by themselves?'" Peter confirmed that Liza's worrying ensured care for their child: "She worries a lot. I'm probably too easygoing, but she makes sure he goes to the doctor, makes sure he has fluoride, makes sure he has all of his immunizations. She's hypervigilant to any time he might be acting sick. She's kind of that way herself. I kid her about being a hypochondriac. She makes sure he gets to bed on time, makes sure he's eating enough, whereas I'm a little more lackadaisical on that."

The two couples described above, like Brendan and Eileen, presented a kind of complementarity or balance between the mother and father — the mother worried, the father didn't — his job, in fact, might be to tell her not to worry. This dynamic reinforced a gendered division of baby worry. Although there was a subtext that the mother's worrying was unnecessary or neurotic, she did not stop. In fact, the suggestion that the mother relax served to reinforce her worrying, because although she did not recognize it as work, she did recognize that worrying got things done for the baby that might not get done if no one worried.

If the father offered to share the worrying rather than telling the mother to stop, the outcome might be quite different. This was suggested to me by my observation that mothers whose husbands spent more time with their babies — and worried more than other fathers did — appeared to worry less than other mothers. But I have too few counterexamples to do anything but speculate about this. Examining another area of mental labor — processing expert information about baby care — further reveals how gendered divisions of mental labor are both an outcome of, and a vehicle for, gender differences in parental consciousness.

Processing Information

The fact that mothers tend to buy and read how-to books on parenting may be directly connected to their being "in charge" of the baby, LaRossa and LaRossa (1989: 144) point out. Because mothers read the books more thoroughly, they are more informed, and both parents assume that the mother will orchestrate and implement the care: "Her purchase of the books reflects what is generally accepted: Babies are 'women's work.'"

There are a number of steps that may be involved in this kind of mental labor:

1. *Deciding on the need for advice*
2. *Locating the advice (often from more than one source)*
3. *Reading/listening to the advice*
4. *Involving/instructing one's partner*
5. *Contemplating and assessing the advice*
6. *Planning for the implementation of the advice*

What I label as steps 1–3 have been found to be done by mothers usually (LaRossa and LaRossa 1989; Hays 1996), even in couples that share parenting (Ehrensaft 1990). Twenty-three out of the twenty-five mothers I interviewed reported reading parenting literature while five of the twenty-five fathers did. Step 4 occurred in a number of variations in the couples I interviewed: mothers told fathers what to read (LaRossa and LaRossa refer to this as "coaxing"); mothers told fathers what they had read; mothers told fathers what to do based on, but without explicit reference to, their own reading:

> *Every once in a while she might pull something out and show me if she found something she thinks I should read, but I usually don't have time. (Jake)*

> *Sarah has read quite a few and I just pretty much go with her. She hasn't really told me I'm doing anything wrong. (Eddie)*

> *He would say, "Well you're the mother, so what's the answer here?" And I said, "What do you think I have that I would*

*know just because I'm the mother?" But I would do a lot
more reading. (Barbara)*

Step 5 — contemplation and assessment of the advice — is often complicated since what women find in advice books is ideology as well as information. Underlying the advice provided by child care experts is an "ideology of intensive mothering" that, among other things, holds individual mothers primarily responsible for child-rearing, and treats mothering as emotionally absorbing, labor intensive, and expert guided (Hays 1996; see also Marshall 1991).[6] Mothers therefore take the responsibility for gathering information from sources that reinforce their primary responsibility for the care of babies; they then have to confront the ideology underlying the advice in order to assess whether they can or want to implement it (Step 6).

The book most relied on by almost three-quarters of the mothers I interviewed who read advice books was *What to Expect the First Year* (Eisenberg, Murkoff, and Hathaway 1989), a book that was conceived to address new mothers' worries. It is explicitly directed to mothers while including only one chapter about becoming a father. Several of the women I interviewed referred to it as their "Bible," and because it is not included in content analyses of expert advice books, I include some excerpts in this chapter (Hays [1996] notes that sales of this book now rival those of T. Berry Brazleton and Penelope Leach, and that the underlying ideology is similar).

What to Expect the First Year was assessed to be a "practical" and "nonjudgmental" guide relative to other advice books in a book review in *The New York Times* (Chira 1994) published on Mother's Day. Yet one of the women I interviewed, a stay-at-home mother who preferred *What to Expect* over other books, nevertheless had questions about what she referred to as its accuracy. Ann Marie's statements were sarcastic in response to the book's advice about the lengths that mothers should go, for example, to see that their babies eat healthy foods: "I like to read *What to Expect*. Although I don't think they're too accurate . . . So your baby should be doing this and the other thing. And never give him any white sugar. Don't give him any cookies. Make sure they're muffins made from fruit juice. Yeah, okay. I'll just pop off in the kitchen and make some muffins."

The book discusses when to introduce solid foods to a baby— something that a father can do whether or not the baby is being breast-fed: "The messages that today's new mother receives about when to start feeding solids are many and confusing . . . . Whom do you listen to? Does mother know best? Or doctor? Or friends?" (Eisenberg, Murkoff, and Hathaway 1989: 202).

This passage illustrates the mental labor that is expected to accompany the introduction of solid foods: choosing when to do it, consulting with others about the issue, and making a decision about whose advice to take. It also presumes that it is the mother who is making the decision in consultation with her mother, doctor, or friends, yet her male partner is not mentioned.

The one chapter addressed to fathers begins with the following question from a presumably typical father: "I gave up a lot of my favorite foods when my wife was pregnant so I could support her efforts to eat right for our baby. But enough's enough. Now that our son's here, shouldn't I be able to eat what I like?" (ibid., 591). The tone of the question suggests that the father is getting guff from someone about his diet. Implication: it may not be only babies whose diets new mothers need to worry about. Regardless of who is nagging this father, the question suggests that fathers may not be independently motivated to eat a healthy diet in the interest of their babies and themselves (although given the comments of Ann Marie, this father may just want some cookies and white sugar in his diet).[7]

As Sharon Hays (1996) points out, authors of advice books may not have created gender differentiation in parenting responsibility, but they certainly play a role in perpetuating it. Mothers I met who already felt that they had the primary responsibility for their babies did not get any disagreement from the advice book they consulted most frequently: "If your husband, for whatever reason, fails to share the load with you, try to understand why this is so and to communicate clearly where you stand. Don't expect him to change overnight, and don't let your resentment when he doesn't trigger arguments and stress. Instead explain, educate, entice; in time, he'll meet you—partway, if not all the way" (ibid., 545).

This advice directs women to do what Arlie Hochschild (1983) refers to as "emotion work" to contain their responses to their husbands' lack of participation. Rather than experiencing stress or anger, new mothers are directed to keep a lid on their feelings and focus on instructing and enticing their husbands into participation (and after all this, not to expect equity).

Managing the Division of Labor

I want to expand the concept of managing that has already been applied to infant care in past studies and suggest that it is not only the baby's appointments and supplies that mothers tend to manage, but their babies' fathers as well (see also Ehrensaft 1990). To use the language from *What to Expect*, "enticing" fathers into helping out with their babies is an invisible mental job performed by new mothers. Liza said, for example: "Peter is very good at helping out. If I say, 'Peter, I'm tired, I'm sick, you've got to do this for me, you've got to do that,' that's fine, he's been more than willing to do that."

Embedded in the use of the verb "help" is the notion that parenting is ultimately the mother's responsibility—that fathers are doing a favor when they parent (McMahon 1995). The default position, which is a factor in mothers' parental consciousness, is that the mother is on duty unless she asks for or is offered help. This is a state of affairs that created dissonance for some of the couples I met, and wives especially, who expected their marriages to be partnerships.

Husbands who reported that they did not do as much caregiving as their wives tended to perceive themselves as helpers to their wives, or as Richard said, the "secondary line of defense." Some fathers expressed guilt about not helping out more, admitting that they simply let their partners do more; some, who became primary caregivers while their wives were at work, relinquished the role upon their wives' return, as in the case of Brendan and Eileen. Even in situations in which fathers reported that they and their partners split tasks equally, mothers often played a role in delegating the work (Coltrane [1989] and Ehrensaft [1990] also describe "manager-helper" dynamics in couples who share child care):

> *I don't change her [diaper] too often—as much as I can get out of it. (Eddie)*

> *She'll hear him when I won't sometimes or whatever, but she doesn't believe me. (Michael)*

> *Then at night either one of us will give him a bath. She'll always give him a bath, or if she can't, she'll tell me to do it because I won't do it unless she tells me, but if she asks me to do it I'll do it. (Peter)*

The commentary from these fathers, who perceived that they split tasks equally with their partners, reflects a division of labor in which their female partners were the ultimate managers. They "shared" tasks with their wives—when their wives told them to.

Diaper changes were a particular area in which the work of enticing was evident:

> *I mean diapering, that's hard to say. He won't volunteer, but if I say, "Honey, she needs a diaper change, could you do it?" he does it. (Whitney)*

> *It took me a little while to get him to change the nasty diapers . . . but now he changes 'em all. He's a pro. (Miranda)*

Mothers also made decisions about when not to delegate:

> *I do diapers. Joel can't handle it well. You know, he does diapers too, but not if there's poop in them. (Maggie)*

I'm pretty much in charge of that, which is fine, because it's really not that big of a deal. And she's more, it seems like she's easier for me than she is for him when it comes to diapering cause I just all the time do it, you know? (Nancy)

Nancy illustrates how habitual patterns can become perceived as making sense — doing becomes a kind of knowing (Daniels 1987; DeVault 1991) — just as being the one to read the book makes the mother the expert. Melissa described what is involved in feeding the baby (and her husband Brett):

I know what has to be done. I know that like when we sit down for dinner, she [child] has to have everything cut up, and then you give it to her, you know, where he sits down and he eats his dinner. Then I have to get everything on the table, get her stuff all done. By the time I'm starting to eat, he's almost finished. Then I have to clean up and I also have to get her cleaned up and I know that like she'll always have to have a bath, and if she has to have a bath and if I need him to give it to her, "Can you do it?" I have to ask . . . because he just wouldn't do it if I didn't ask him. You know, it's just assumed that he doesn't have to do it.

While on one level it appears that women are in charge of the division of labor, the assumption of female responsibility means that, on another level, men are in charge — because it is only with their permission and cooperation that mothers can relinquish their duties. Maggie complained that Joel would leave the house while their child was taking a nap: "It's always the father that can just say, 'Okay, I'm gonna go.' Well I obviously can't leave, he's ready for a nap, you know? It's nap time. Mommy seems to always have to stay. I think that fathers have more freedom."

These kinds of statements go against suggestions that mothers may not want to relinquish control to their male partners because motherhood is a source of power for women. It may be more accurate to speak, as Coltrane (1996: 230) does, of some mothers trying to hold on to control and self-esteem by maintaining their primary responsibility for family work. I also think that the desire of mothers to be perceived as good mothers is quite powerful, and this may be what they feel they are trading off if they are not the primary caregivers. Children validate women's characters, McMahon (1995: 234) argues: "For a woman to be remiss in feeling responsible for her child would implicate her whole moral character." Note that McMahon talks about what the woman feels, not what she does.

In the context of feeling that they were ultimately responsible for their children, the women I interviewed were often satisfied with their partners' willingness to help and appreciated gestures from their husbands. Gloria, for example, talked about Jay bringing a bottle upstairs for their son before leaving for work in the morning. Mandy, another stay-at-home mother, spoke with appreciation about Chip not "holding it against" her when she goes out with friends: "He never says, 'Go, but I'm gonna remember this.' He doesn't ever do that."

When mothers delegated tasks to their husbands, men's compliance with orders was not compulsory (see also DeVault 1991). Fathers who considered themselves equal participants in the division of labor would use the fact that they were willing to do diapers as an example:

> We each will do whatever we have to do. It's not like I won't change diapers. (Chad)

> We tried to make it pretty equally divided. I mean I don't have any aversion to doing diapers or any of that kind of stuff. (David)

Mothers did not necessarily see any baby task as optional for them, as Sarah illustrated: "It's kind of give and take. As far as diaper changing, I think I do more . . . It's not one of his favorite tasks."

In the separation of mental and physical care of babies, women were the "bosses" in the sense that they created the organizational plan and delegated tasks to their partners. But they managed without the privileges of paid managers. If their "workers" did not do the job, they blamed themselves:

> *I think I myself have a problem with relationships, with trusting, and I'm afraid to trust that he would get the things done that need to be done. But you know, I think he probably would. (Maggie)*

> *I guess I'm not demanding enough. (Ann Marie)*

> *I tend to get his stuff ready for day care and Sean could do it very easily. It's just a pattern. Part of it is my problem that I don't say, "You do it tonight." (Sylvia)*

Some women just preferred to absorb the tasks themselves rather than train and compensate their partners. Mothers may not want to pay the price of having fathers help more, Ralph and Maureen LaRossa (1989: 146) suggest: "They may not be comfortable with the deferential stance they are expected to take to offset their husband's gratuities." Ironically, carrying the primary and ultimate responsibility for baby care may disempower women in relation to their husbands—leading to greater, rather than less, dependence and losses in interpersonal and economic power (Waldron and Routh 1981; Blumberg and Coleman 1989).

Where does the assumption that women are the default parents come from? And why do some mothers become stressed by their apparent primacy to children? The next chapter explores intersections between parental consciousness and modern cultural imagery of what it means to be a good mother and father.

❦

CHAPTER 3

"Good" Mothers and Fathers

WHEN WE LEFT BRENDAN AND EILEEN IN CHAP-ter 2, they were both asserting that Eileen experi-enced more guilt and anxiety than Brendan did, while fathering for Brendan was simply "fun." Why did Eileen and Brendan have different experiences of becoming parents? Why did they approach the work of caregiving differently (Eileen want-ing to do more and Brendan happy with doing less)? Why was Eileen anxious and Brendan having fun? Eileen suggested a dif-ference between them that was sociological in nature, and one that I argue is underrated as an influence on transitions into parenthood.

Eileen's suggestion dealt with the content of social images or "models" that she perceived for mothers and fathers. In describ-ing her impression of "the good mother image," Eileen said, "Well she's somehow all nurturing and all present and always there." Eileen's parental consciousness was influenced by her be-lief that, although she wished to, she could not match this image: "I'm not even going to be able to have a shot at it [conforming to the good mother image] because I'm not a lot of those things."

Eileen talked about how women cannot possibly meet the model for mothers while it is not difficult for men to exceed what she perceived as the model for fathers: "There's no way I can meet the model, even though it's there. It's very easy for a man to exceed the model, right? I mean by some [standards], Brendan happens to do a whole lot, but I know some friends of ours who will do minimal things and everybody kind of does handstands for them." The model for men, as she saw it, was the breadwinner and "stability provider": "So I think if you [a father] can figure out a way to do both, plus some other nurturing or care-providing activities, you have a real opportunity to exceed the model."

Fathers could easily do better than what is expected of them, Eileen felt, and mothers could only do worse. Not only were the messages for mothers unattainable, but they were confusing and contradictory. She told a story about a visit to her parents, during which Jimmy was being clingy: "He wouldn't go to anybody else but me. My father said, 'Look at her, she's spoiling him.' And my mother said, 'Be quiet . . . she ought to be glad he knows who she is.'" She described her parents' statements as "guilt converging from both points." She told them, "I'm scared to death I'm spoiling this kid every time I'm with him, and that he knows how to manipulate me. And I'm also scared to death he's going to forget who he is, who I am."

"Yeah, there are still expectations for mothers," she concluded after telling this story. When I asked how these expectations fit into Eileen's own ideas, she said, "I buy into them. I absolutely do."

Eileen's internalization of a good mother image that she could not live up to was in stark contrast to Brendan's internal experience. When I asked him whether he thinks there are social expectations for fathers, he said, "Probably more expectations for mothers." When I asked him what those are, he replied, "They're more responsible for children." Brendan wasn't worried about being a "good" father in the way that Eileen was conscious of whether she was a "good" mother. Eileen's perception was that if Brendan *had* worried, he would have measured up fine. The fact that she could not say the same about herself, as Eileen suggested, is partly

a sociological phenomenon; it reflects the different social experiences and expectations confronted by new mothers and fathers.

THE SOCIAL CONSTRUCTION
OF GENDERED PARENTHOOD

There has not been a lot of research about whether new parents are aware of and think about social expectations for mothers
and fathers. Perhaps this is because of the difficulty of defining
"society" as a concrete object (Lemert 1995). However, when I
asked new parents what they thought society expected of mothers
and fathers, they did not ask me what I was referring to — they
answered my question. Society "is not anything we can feel,
smell, touch, see, or hear — at least not directly," Charles Lemert
(1995: 15) writes, yet "we can think it, talk about it, and use it . . .
in order to explain the lives we and others lead."

The parents I interviewed thought about, talked about, and
used their perceptions of social expectations as reference points
in their parenting. They did not all have the same views of what
society expects of mothers and fathers, but none disputed that
social norms do exist for parents. Although they didn't necessarily
conform to these expectations, they thought about them; they
were part of their consciousness. And this, in turn, shaped their
experiences and interactions as couples. Brendan didn't get up in
the middle of the night, in part because Eileen thought that she
should. He didn't experience his employment as interfering with
their baby's care, in part because Eileen perceived hers that way.
Brendan had fun, in part because Eileen was anxious. And Eileen
was anxious, in part because she did not conform to an image of
"good" mothering that she claimed to absolutely buy into.

Perhaps more than any other aspect of gender, mothering
is perceived as "natural, universal, and unchanging," Evelyn
Nakano Glenn (1994: 3) suggests. To be a mother, and to mother
in a particular way, is an essential part of social definitions of
womanhood. One explanation, therefore, for why new parents
sustain differentiated images of mothering and fathering, is be-

cause they feel accountable to these already established images and "to normative conceptions regarding the essential womanly nature of child care" (West and Fenstermaker 1993: 165).[1]

For a woman not to be preoccupied with her baby might challenge her social definition as a mother (and as a woman). For a man to be preoccupied with his baby, rather than with his duty as an economic provider, might call into question his social definition as a father and as a man. In a hypothetical game of "chicken," in which the winner is the parent who can wait longer for the other parent to take responsibility for a baby's needs, it is difficult for mothers not to lose. Ruth said of what it means to be "the wife and mother": "If I hear him [baby] cry during the night, I'm more apt to get right up than Jake. Or if it's time to get up in the morning and I hear him, I'm more apt to get up and go get him. Jake is more apt to stay in bed and see what happens."

Wives and mothers, according to Ruth, do not wait to see if their male partner will take care of the baby. McMahon (1995: 159) writes in her study of mothers, "Dominant representations of woman's character . . . so tie women to caring, and in particular to caring for their own children, that it becomes unthinkable for a woman not to act in a responsible way toward her child—to be an irresponsible mother." For mothers, there is a much greater threat to their identities than there is for fathers if, at any particular moment, they are not taking care of their baby.

Whether mothers actually think about their babies all the time or not, they are held accountable to this expectation. Alison, for example, reminded herself that she *should* be worried about her baby while she was at her job or she would be a bad mother. Since fathers' accountability lies outside of direct baby care and interaction, their attention to their babies may be moderated or suppressed. As anyone who has held a baby knows, there is dissonance in acknowledging the pleasure of that experience while also feeling that one's responsibility is away from that baby. Wade expressed a sense of loss about things he missed with his baby, but he said, "it kind of goes back to the idea of being a father," which was to support his family economically.

This is, many social analysts have argued, the dominant cultural norm for a father — that he is "not directly important, only indirectly as protector and provider of the mother-child couplet" (Rapoport et al. 1977: 35). While motherhood is perceived as "a constant and exclusive responsibility," fatherhood is equated with breadwinning, an activity distant from the day-to-day nurture of children (Thompson and Walker 1989: 860). In more stark language, Coltrane (1996: 4) suggests that mothering "implies ongoing care and nurturing of children" while fathering "has typically implied an initial sex act and the financial obligation to pay."

Some of the new parents I interviewed perceived these differentiated images of mothers and fathers as still dominant in society. Others saw a change toward the expectation that mothers be employed and fathers be more directly involved with their children. Despite these apparent changes, however, new parents' own images of good parenting reflected gender-differentiated models of mothers as ever-present nurturers and of fathers as providers and part-time playmates.

I think that these more intractable images — the kind that Eileen described in her discussion of the good mother — are powerful in shaping mothers' and fathers' different parental consciousness because they are more deep-seated and contradict apparent changes in behavioral expectations for mothers and fathers. As we will see, many of the mothers I interviewed perceived that society expects them to "do it all," yet their own image of what it means to be a good mother is to "always be there" for the baby. Many fathers felt that they are expected to be involved with their babies as well as to provide for them, but the actual level of involvement is unclear. What is clear is that the father provides economically for the baby.

There is a sociohistorical context for the association of mothers with physically present nurturing and of fathers with absent economic provision. In the eighteenth century, motherhood was not particularly emphasized and "child rearing was neither a discrete nor an exclusively female task . . . both parents were simply advised to 'raise up' their children together" (Margolis 1984: 12). But norms changed with industrialization in the nineteenth century. As manufacturing took paid work out of individual households, the "public" sphere of the economy and state became perceived as a male sphere with economic provision the job of fathers, while women were left (at least ideologically if not in actuality) to the "private" domain of the household and children (see Coltrane 1996; Glenn 1994; Osmond and Thorne 1993).

More than any other cultural belief, Coltrane (1996: 25) argues, the idealized notion of separate spheres for mothers and fathers continues to shape "what it means to be a man or a woman in our society." It is not surprising then that new parents would be accountable to this imagery. As Miranda said, "I'm supposed to do what I'm doing just because I'm the mom."

With industrialization, middle-class wives, whose husbands were absent from the domestic sphere in a new way, were urged to devote themselves to parenting full-time. The mother-child relationship became perceived as exclusive, its centrality inevitable and natural. This change in ideology about motherhood was part of a general orientation toward making a science of the domestic world. The home became industrialized as the world outside of it did. As scientific principles evolved that were designed to make workers in factories more productive, parallel rhetoric emerged in relation to efficiency in the home. And, as other productive activities moved out of the home, children began to be perceived as a project in themselves rather than as integrated participants in family work (Ehrenreich and English 1978).

Child-rearing "experts" perpetuated the notion that mothering is an all-engulfing activity, while also suggesting that mothers were at great risk of doing it wrong. Although any diversion of their attention away from their children defined mothers as "rejecting," too much mothering resulted in "overprotection." Some experts even suggested that overprotection was simply disguised aggression toward children (Ehrenreich and English 1978). The residue of these mixed messages is apparent in Eileen's story about the visit to her parents, during which they suggested both that she was "smothering" her child and that "she should be glad he knows her."

Although baby care experts such as Dr. Benjamin Spock appeared to become less judgmental about maternal employment and to reinforce the role of fathers during the 1970s (Margolis 1984), Hays (1996: 55) argues that expert advice has changed more in form than in content. She points out, for example, that current editions of *Dr. Spock's Baby and Child Care* undermine gender-neutral language "when he suggests that the 'parent' buy 'a new dress' or go to the 'beauty parlor' if child-rearing is giving (him or) her the blues." There is still implicit in baby care advice an ideology of "intensive mothering" to which mothers (across their many differences) continue to respond (Hays 1996). "Intensive mothering" refers to a style of child rearing in which individual mothers are responsible for nurturing children in a way that requires much time, energy, and money.

For several parents that I interviewed, ideology related to motherhood was referred to as an image of "the perfect mother," although the specific imagery associated with perfection varied. Maggie described her image of the perfect mother:

> *See like if I were the perfect mother I'd be home every day. Get up with my son, you know, do breakfast, a nice breakfast with bath and then we'd have outdoor activities, you know, we'd go to the park and feed the ducks or you know, every day would be like that [laughs]. And then you'd have your nice scheduled naptime and snack, and you know, you'd do something like artsy craftsy, make something, and teach your child, I don't know. Then have dinner on the table and the house would be clean. That's like the perfect mother image, you know?*

Sean described the mother who "does it all": "Well let's see. Warm and loving and there all the time . . . The perfect mother knows the right thing to say for comfort but also has to have a career, bring something to the board room that changes everybody's mind and makes a lot of money. 'Here's a better way to make cookies.' 'By God, she's right!' I think that mothers are expected to be both those things now and very good at it, and if they're not, if they're at all human, there's something wrong."

Whitney didn't know what the perfect mother is; she just knew that "everyone" expects her to be one: "In today's world, I tell you, I think that everyone expects you to be like the perfect mother." When I asked her what the perfect mother is, she replied, "I don't know. I mean if I knew, I would be one."

Whitney's confusion about what defines the perfect mother resonates with nationally representative research cited by Coltrane (1996: 26) that suggests that women are expected to be both "generous self-sacrificing mothers" as well as "dedicated professionals." As Alison said, "I think society's pretty confused right now. Working mothers, day care, I don't think they know what, society is confused I think."

Even though both the traditional mother and "the supermom" are generally considered socially acceptable, Hays (1996: 132) suggests that "their coexistence represents a serious cultural ambivalence about how mothers should behave." Some of the mothers and fathers I interviewed spoke to these mixed messages:

I think it is really conflicting and I think it is really making it hard on women. Actually I think that there is no one thing anymore. If being an at-home mother is so good, why is it such a demeaning job to admit that you're a homemaker? But then again, if you're out working and having this great career, then that lessens you as a mother . . . I think we basically give parents a double-edged sword. Well stay at home and you'll have this great baby but you're not much of a person. (Gloria)

Well there certainly seems to be a strain about this. Motherhood is supposed to be the be-all and end-all for a woman, her defining role in life. At the same time, there seems to

*be something out there saying that just being a mother
isn't enough. You need to be a mother and have a job and
have a career and jog in the morning, learn a foreign language. (Phil)*

It was notable how often the mothers I talked to described
social expectations for mothers as something different from what
they themselves were doing (see also Cowan and Cowan [1992:
114], who note that *every* woman in their sample worried that she
made the wrong choice in her work/family arrangements). Some
of the mothers who were employed perceived the social expectation to be caretaking at home full-time. On the other hand, one
stay-at-home mother, Constance, talked about society devaluing
motherhood as a job: "Oh there's definitely still the image of
mothers that are at home, no question — that they're just watching
TV and having a good time, going shopping and stuff."

The most prevalent image described by the new mothers I
interviewed was the mother who can do it all, or as more than
one person said, "bring home the bacon and fry it up in the pan":

*That's the way I think society views it, that you're a good
mom if you can do it all. You've got the kids, you've got the
baby-sitter and you do the nine to five, you come home and
cook the dinner and clean your house and you just do it all.
And I can't do it all like that. (Miranda)*

*It's like the mother is expected to take care of the child, you
know, but not necessarily stay at home because she is also
expected to work, but sort of like be superwoman, you know,
and do everything. And then if one area is lacking, it's your
job or whatever, she is reprimanded there, and if something
happens with her child where he's getting into trouble or
something, it's because she is not doing a good enough job as
a mother. (Margaret)*

A good portion of the parents I interviewed felt that mothers
are now expected to work for pay, but without any corresponding

changes in their responsibilities at home. One father said, "It's okay for the mother to work as long as she maintains that child care." It was also suggested that the money women make is less important than men's contributions. Harriet said, "The husband is the provider and the wife's income is kind of secondary. Oh I know there are probably quite a few of them out there that make more money than their husbands, but I still think that the father is like the head of the household."

Interestingly, while mothers thought they were supposed to "do it all," the most prevalent response from fathers was that society expected mothers to be homemakers, nurturers, and caretakers; as Eddie said, "wait on the baby hand and foot." The fathers I spoke with were more likely than mothers to separate financial and emotional caretaking in discussing social expectations for mothers. Peter said, for example: "A good mother would be very caring, nurturing, sounds very sexist, doesn't it? The societal image of a good mother would be one who gets along well with her husband, is always there for the kids to help primarily I would guess emotionally rather than financially."

Yet some fathers whose wives were primarily at home tended to perceive this as an arrangement that is not supported by society, as Bill's commentary illustrates: "There I think it maybe changed a little bit where a good mother is one that can juggle a career and raising a kid, which I don't agree with that, because I can't see sending your kid off to a baby-sitter for eight hours a day . . . That's the way I see like society seeing what a good mom is, but I don't agree." The need for these fathers to defend arrangements in which mothers stayed at home reflects the cultural ambivalence identified by Hays (1996).

While the manifest societal messages that many of the parents I interviewed perceived were that men and women are equal and that mothers are allowed to be employed, the more latent imagery they carried reflected gendered expectations of difference in how available and nurturing mothers and fathers should be. When the question shifted from what society expects of mothers to their own images of "good" mothers, mothers talked less about the home versus employment debate and more about an image of caregiving and commitment that is instinctive and exclusive. Hays (1996) notes also that although the group of mothers she studied tended to identify strongly as either employed or stay-at-home mothers, both groups attempted to resolve their feelings of inadequacy by returning to the logic of the ideology of intensive mothering. The answers of many of the parents I spoke with to the question of what their own image is of a good mother revealed foremost a concern for a kind of selfless presence — being "there all the time" and focused on the child:

> *She is attentive to Dylan, you know, she puts Dylan first. If she wants to read a book and Dylan wants to play, she'll put the book down. (Jay)*

> *She spends countless and countless and countless hours of doing nothing but nurturing Jerry's needs. (Todd)*

When I asked mothers if there was anyone in particular they thought of as an example of their own image of a good mother, images of instinct, availability, and self-control often appeared:

> *[About a sister] It was like she was born to know that that's what she wanted to do. (Melissa)*

> *[About a mother] She always just had the right things to say and cares so much and . . . the love was always there, it was always there, it was unconditional . . . She was always there, always there to support and always there to, never to criticize, always there to encourage growth, encourage everything we ever did. (Liza)*

> *[About a babysitter] She never yells, she never gets upset, even if her kids are doing something wrong. Her kids are the most well-behaved children I have ever met in my life and I think it has a lot to do with her. She doesn't work and spends all that time with her children. Her house is spotless no matter*

when I come over. She's very good with her house and her kids. (Whitney)

Whitney's comments about her baby-sitter not working and being very good with her house and her children reveal a constellation of behaviors associated with good mothering that is linked to the historically and culturally specific notion of a separation of domestic and public spheres. Whether women define themselves as employed or not tends to be a touchstone for more latent expectations about their service and availability to their families.[2]

On the other hand, some of the people I interviewed revised this notion of good mothering; and Collins (1987: 5) notes that African American women "have long integrated their activities as economic providers into their mothering relationships." In the group of white parents that I interviewed, women and men who had been raised by single mothers were particularly likely to acknowledge economic roles as a part of mothering. In talking about his mother who had provided for three children on her own, Stuart said: "Whether she was good or not, she did as good as she could." (It is striking that Stuart acknowledged that there might be a question about whether his mother would be considered "good" in culturally dominant terms.) Elliot expressed a similar sentiment to Stuart's—that his mother had done the best she could: "I know that my mom did everything she could . . . I look at the things I had now and I don't know how the hell she did it, you know, I mean I really don't—to be supporting my sister and I."

For Nancy, her mother's ability to support her family on her own led her to associate caring with strength: "We didn't have a lot of money but she just loved us very, very much. She worked sometimes three jobs but she took care of us three kids and I just see that strongness and I really respect that and admire that."

The image that these adult children of single mothers had of what their mothers did to support their children is more commonly associated with fatherhood, which focuses on economic provision (see Thompson and Walker 1989). Although a majority of fathers in national surveys say that they should be directly involved in their children's lives, they don't necessarily follow through, and the most common justification is that their jobs interfere (Coltrane 1996).

Several of the parents I interviewed suggested that societal expectations for fathers are less strong than they are for mothers (and a few thought that they are nonexistent). Of whether there are social expectations for fathers, Brett said, "I think there used to be but I think it kind of got lost with families not being two-parent families." I asked him what he thought it used to be, and he answered, "When I was growing up it was the father was the provider, the mother was the home, took care of the home. The father did Little League and did whatever. I don't know. I'd like to see that it's coming back that way but I'm not sure it is."

Part of what Brett is nostalgic for is the clarity of a gendered division of labor. Robert Griswold (1993: 4, 9) argues in his history of fatherhood in America that "nothing has changed and continues to change fatherhood more than the collapse of men's monopoly on breadwinning." Fatherhood has become politicized, Griswold notes: "its terms are contested, its significance fragmented, its meaning unstable." This ambiguity came through in the commentary of the parents I interviewed, although perhaps in response to a sense of fatherhood as an institution in flux, many of them continued to ground their vision of fathering in economic provision.

In contrast to the lofty expectations for mothers, Ken said that what society expects of fathers is "being a provider for the family and just . . . not abusing your family in any way." Mandy argued that people are more suspicious of fathers, and perceive them as disciplinarians who "need their time away and . . . are not always there" for their children: "And that's really a bad stereotype because most fathers out there I think just love their children to death. They just love them." Yet Mandy didn't think that society equated love with fathering.[3]

Breadwinning was the most prevalent social expectation for fathers identified by the mothers I interviewed. It is notable that, among the parents I spoke to, the women perceived traditional expectations for fathers in the same way that the men did for mothers. Samantha commented, "I think the social image of a good father is more about how much money the father makes and what kind of job he has than whether he's actually there and paying attention and spending time with his children."

Some fathers made a link between the expectation that fathers should provide economically and the cost of this expectation (in terms of their ability to be physically present to their babies). As Wade said, "I felt like I was missing out on a lot of stuff. It would be nice to be there to see a lot of what is going on, but on the other hand, it kind of goes back to the idea of being a father. Well this is what people do. This is life . . . I would guess society probably still looks at the father being the breadwinner and being more of a support function I would think."

Todd felt that he didn't conform to what society expects of fathers because his wife earned more money than he did: "I think too many people depend on fathers for work . . . Peggy works, sometimes she works a lot more hours than I do and does bring in the bread . . . I don't think . . . a certain amount of money makes a good father. That's one thing that society puts on fathers today."

The norm that Todd perceived society "puts on fathers today" — responsibility for breadwinning — evolved with industrialization, when men's productive work moved out of the domestic sphere and their involvement with children became more distant (Coltrane 1996; Pleck 1987). The "father as breadwinner" model socializes men toward jobs and away from family care. However, variations on this model have been emerging, largely in response to trends in women's labor force participation as well as to the rise of the welfare state (Benson 1968; Pleck 1981; Pleck 1987). It is no longer always assumed that fathers can or will be financially responsible for the care of their children. Nor is it assumed that fathers are incapable of nurturing children. Finally, there continues to be a belief that the influence of mothers *should* be tempered by fathers.[4]

Some of the fathers I interviewed reflected Coltrane's argument (1996: 5) that it is becoming fashionable for fathers to act more like mothers—to be "nurturing family men rather than the distant providers and protectors they once were." As Bill observed:

> *I think it's changed. You know when I was little and my dad was a dad when I was growing up I think it was more just go out and earn the money, come home, pay the bills, and you're a good dad, you know? And I think maybe I got that a little bit in my head because maybe I overemphasize that . . . And now it's more that you've got to change the diapers and you've got to feed her and you've got to do things with him or her, you know, when they're young . . . you've got to be a lot more involved.*

Some mothers also perceived a change, as Laura did: "I think people look at involvement to see a good father, somebody who takes the time to be with their family. Somebody who finds some kind of time no matter what it is."

One father talked about not enjoying fatherhood as much as he thought he should: "In one sense it seems like there is an image of parenting as women who are supposed to take care of the kids and fathers are at work or out in the garage puttering . . . On the other hand, I certainly got the impression that you're supposed to find fatherhood wonderful."

Phil talked about himself as not having the level of "paternal instinct" that he thought he should because he was not happy with the changes that fatherhood has made in his life. This was a father, however, whose wife was very happy with their division of child care; but as one father in Ehrensaft's (1990: 52) study of sharing parents points out, there may be negative implications for those fathers whose arrangements are more egalitarian: "Sometimes my son gets me when I don't want to be with him. He gets my resentments. In conventional families men are with the children when they *want* to be with them." And in "conventional" families, women are the ones with whom the buck stops, which is probably a factor in their different experiences of the transition.

Has fatherhood changed or not? Some people argue that the culture of fatherhood has changed more quickly than the conduct of it (LaRossa 1988) — people are talking the talk about a new fatherhood more than they are walking the walk. National data suggest that the transition to parenthood "still has greater implications for changing married women's daily routines than men's" — that contemporary fatherhood has not changed mothers' primary responsibility (Sanchez and Thomson 1997: 759). Perhaps there is more than one "culture" of fatherhood, as Griswold (1993: 267) suggests: "Lamaze coaches and deadbeat dads, daddy trackers and child deserters, wildmen and wimps, new fathers and old patriarchs, they are all part of American culture and the politics of gender." For the new parents I interviewed, what this looked like was an ambiguity about how much hands-on parenting is necessary for a man to be perceived as an involved father, and how much involvement is necessary for a father to be deemed "good." Some argued not much:

> He doesn't have to take part in raising the kids or something, but he just has to be there . . . play catch with their sons or build a doll house for their daughters. (Michael)

> Someone that takes the children out, you know, on the weekends and teaches his son to play catch. But then again it isn't as close as the mother is because well in most situations I think the mother spends more time with the children. A lot of times you see on the TV and stuff the father is always too busy for the children because of work or whatever. . . . Fathers are more supposed to be the disciplinarian I think. I don't really know why that is. But that's the impression I get is that the father is the one that does the grounding and stuff. (Jay)

While some mothers thought that fathers' roles are definitely changing — "they don't think twice about walking a stroller now," Constance said — others, including Miranda, did not: "I notice when I'm out in public, if I see a father carrying a baby around on his shoulders or just pushing the stroller or anything, I notice it's really uncommon. I always see the mom pushing the stroller."

And some mothers, like Sylvia, argued that change is not coming quickly enough: "I think it is changing but I think that fathers are there to play . . . I don't know, I guess I'd like to think it's changing but I don't think it's changing as fast as it should be, you know? There's not enough accommodations at this point for fathers although it's starting with paternity leave and things like that. So I guess I feel that fathers tend to play a more supportive, secondary role in the family."

Some mothers suggested that men are taken off the hook when it comes to the less glamorous parts of parenting:

> *I think usually people think, well, we'll let that slide, he's a man . . . that's just the way they are and they can't handle children. It's not a man's job anyway. It's the mother's job to get the child ready and off to wherever . . . the poor man, you know, it's hard for the man. You've got to bitch to give him a challenge. (Maggie)*

> *They are the ones that get to take the kids to the park. They are not the ones that have to sit there and feed them for an hour and a half and scrape the yogurt off the walls. (Gloria)*

While mothers struggle with a cultural model of maternal presence that many feel they can't match, fathers exceed the model of father absence relatively easily. These discrepancies play a role in the gender conflict stimulated by transitions into parenthood. Mothers are confused about what is expected of them, and whatever they are doing feels wrong. Expectations for fathers seem more consistent, on one hand, and less absolute on the other, in terms of their direct contact with children (see Gerson [1991] on breadwinning as compulsory for fathers). Some of the mothers I interviewed described conflict over whether they would be perceived as loving enough, yet fathers who were loving at all got high marks. While mothers perceived they were expected to "do it all," fathers who did anything were considered to be good fathers. Maddy suggested that people take mothers' interactions with their children for granted while fathers get a lot more encouragement and credit for doing things that go unrecognized in mothers: "We're going to be flying out west . . . and I read somewhere that a mother with a crying baby is an object of disdain where the father is an object of sympathy . . . I think people, when they see a father supporting a baby [by] helping them walk, picking them up, wiping a tear — it's just one of those things they make Kodak moments out of, and it's more the sort of thing that you expect of women, I think, so it wouldn't elicit the same response."

Maddy was critical of this double standard, but it was acceptable to other parents with whom I spoke. Stuart talked about what he does to be a good father: "I try not to, although Laura may do more, I try not to just sit around and watch while she does everything." For Maggie, Joel's willingness simply to be on call and go against the ribbing of his friends made him a good father: "Whenever he goes out, he calls. His friends call him—you don't want to know what they call him—'Yeah, you gotta call home.' But he still does anyway. And that's a good father."

Other mothers commented on their partners' willingness to be what Phil referred to as "the secondary line of defense":

> He's always here if I need him. I can call him from work if I need something. If I had a bad day and say, "take her," he does. He takes her to the park. He will just do things on his own with her. (Whitney)

> I think that Peter, using him as an example: helping me out when I come home, playing with the baby . . . getting up in the morning with him . . . and also in terms of emotional support, well I think a lot of it is the emotional because we're both working, just helping out with the care. (Liza)

The fathers I interviewed seemed more clear than mothers were about what they ultimately were supposed to do for their children. Although the amount of hands-on care was ambiguous, the images new parents described of "good" fathers tended to be more consistently matched with what they perceived social expectations to be than the images of "good" mothers were. For example, some fathers thought that fathers were expected to provide financially, and this was their own image of a good father:

> *Someone who can financially take care of the family . . . so the mother can be — now it sounds male chauvinist — but Melissa has always wanted to stay home so I want to make sure that she can do that. (Brett)*

> *I do think in a traditional sense where I'm the father, I'm the husband, it's my job to support the family. (Wade)*

Some mothers also talked about paid work as an important part of fathering, using their own fathers as examples. In the following cases, one daughter described a preindustrial-sounding vision of her childhood on a farm in which her father's work and parenting roles were integrated. The second example was a more typical scenario of paid work taking a father out of actual contact with his child:

> *He was always around but he was always working but very often I'd go out into the barn and find my dad and he always had time to include me in his work if it was something safe. (Sarah)*

> *He worked fifteen-sixteen hours a day but I still think he was a perfect dad because the reason he was working is to pay for everything that I needed and wanted. (Miranda)*

When I spoke to fathers about people in their lives who personified their images of "good" fathers, they focused on things fathers do for children, rather than on the constant presence emphasized in discussions of good mothering:

> *[About a grandfather] Well he worked real hard . . . and he taught me a lot about fishing. (Tom)*

[About a grandfather] He's done, you know, little things like go to my baseball games and things like that, taught me how to hunt and fish and that. Just the little things that mean a lot after a while. (Joel)

[About a father] I try to pattern myself after him. You know, he's the type of person, especially now that he does have more money, who will do anything for you. Not that money is the be-all and end-all of everything but it does help out if you do get into a situation or whatever. (Bill)

The theme of what fathers do for children was also present when mothers in this sample talked about their images of good fathers. Beth said of her husband and child: "He plays with her and likes to take her places, show her nature things, things outside, lizards and frogs and stuff." Maggie's vision of a good father also focused on doing: "teaching him, reading him bedtime stories, giving him a bath." Brendan summed it up best perhaps when he said to me in a recent follow-up interview: "To be a good father, that's the easiest standard. Well, how many things did I do for my kid? You can just count: bing bing bing bing."

Mothers characterized their husbands as good fathers even when they were conscious of "imperfections" that were components of the images of good mothers, such as being patient and loving with children's tears. Maddy said of Phil, "He makes Louise laugh. He's willing to spend quite a bit of time playing with her. He's not necessarily real patient with the tears and stuff, but there aren't that many of those."

When some of the mothers talked about their image of good fathers, what they seemed to appreciate as much as the level of involvement was when there appeared to be no compulsion or obligation evident in the involvement:

He's completely devoted to her [child]. He's completely devoted to me. And you know we have a hard time sometimes because I don't feel he helps as much as he should but he loves to just go off and snuggle with her . . . No one's ever said you have to be devoted to them. That's just the way he grew up though. (Melissa)

A good father is someone who really cares, does everything he can for his family because he wants to, not because he feels he has to. (Nancy)

We have good friends that I think her husband is a great father . . . I mean he won't even ask if she wants to sleep late. He'll just get up with the kids without even thinking about it. (Gloria)

The differentiation between maternal "being" and paternal "doing" that Ehrensaft (1990) identifies is present in the cultural imagery associated with good mothering and fathering to which the parents I interviewed were accountable. Good mothers *are*, as Eileen noted, nurturing, present, and always there. Good fathers *do*, as Brendan remarked, "bing bing bing bing."

The New News and the Old

The new parents that I interviewed were aware of and responsive to cultural norms and imagery surrounding motherhood and fatherhood. And although they perceived changes from the nineteenth century ideology of separate spheres for mothers and fathers, the imagery that they carried of good parenting continued to reflect differentiated expectations for women and men that are reflected in national trends toward more gender-traditional than egalitarian divisions of labor, especially once women and men become parents (Sanchez and Thomson 1997). The new parents I met did not necessarily all conform to this differentiation in their own parenting arrangements, but motherhood and fatherhood — in whatever forms mothers and fathers do them — convey something about gender (Griswold 1993).

Where do new parents learn what it means to be a good

mother or father, husband or wife? And why do dichotomized images persist, despite what many perceive as changes in social expectations for mothers and fathers? While I can't presume to know the origin of these images for any individual person, I will suggest that they are continuously reproduced on both an interactional and an institutional level. That is, although some of the people I interviewed were embarrassed about the situation, some denied it, and some wanted it different, gender dichotomy continues to be embedded in social interaction and structure, and the transition into parenthood is a particular point at which these dynamics are visible.

Every day, men and women in my study were having interactions with each other, friends, coworkers, family members, child care providers, and simply other members of their gender that suggested that men and women have different forms and levels of responsibility for families. They interpreted and made decisions about their own approaches to parenting in the context of these interactions. The messages that new parents experience in their routine interactions are also reinforced through institutions or social structures with which new parents come in contact—hospitals, families, workplaces, child care settings, and the media—as we will see in later chapters. Some parents will describe their vulnerability to what medical and expert personnel told them was most "natural" for their babies. A father will talk about how badly he felt that his boss did not give him time off when his baby was born. A mother will describe the discrepancy she feels between her own life and the messages "they" convey in the media.

Both the amorphous "they" with which parents I met referred to social structures and institutions and the "they" that parents know by name convey messages about how "real" women and men are supposed to do gender, marriage, and parenthood. The rest of this book explores interactional and institutional processes that serve as enforcement mechanisms for the reproduction of gender differentiation in new parents' transitions into parenthood.

❧

CHAPTER 4

Bonding with the Baby:
Biology and Social Meanings

I WAS INTERESTED IN FINDING OUT HOW THE MEAN-
ings that the new parents I interviewed ascribed to biological sex differences intersected with their approaches to parenthood. This chapter describes connections between gendered
transitions into parenthood and interpretations of biological sex
differences. I focus this discussion on postpartum biological phenomena, although obviously the first difference between mothers
and fathers is that women get pregnant, carry, and give birth to
babies — and men do not.

For some people, the tendency for mothers to be primary caregivers to babies has an explanation that is self-evident: women are
biologically different from men. In this view, women are innately
more nurturing than men, and that is why they take more responsibility for babies (see summary in LaRossa 1986). Others dispute
this view, however, presenting evidence that fathers are as competent at nurturing infants as mothers are (Parke and Sawin 1976;
Parke 1981). A related debate is whether differing approaches to
children are programmed into mothers and fathers by evolution.
Some people argue that women are "wired" to be more invested

in individual children because they can't produce as many in their lifetimes as men can, while men withhold their investment because they have the potential to have many more offspring (see discussion of Lancaster's work in Belsky and Kelly 1994). Yet while anthropologists describe the pervasiveness of gendered divisions of labor in many, and perhaps all, societies, biologist Anne Fausto-Sterling (1985: 198) notes: "The problem is that no two societies have exactly the *same* form. What's good for the gander in one culture is just fine for the goose in another. . . . The division of labor by sex embodies a seeming contradiction: it is a human universal but it has no universal meaning."

Another approach to the division of baby care — the biosocial approach — combines an assertion of biological differences between the caregiving capacities of women and men with the observation that societies will ascribe more or less meaning and consequences to these differences. In this view, biological and cultural factors interact in determining male and female parenting roles (see Rossi 1985; Udry 1994). I am not sure how anyone can make the argument that any human behavior is clearly "nature" as opposed to "nurture" — or the other way around. What I suspect is that both matter, but it is virtually impossible to know how, since we have both biological and social experiences before we even get out of the womb.

To argue that there is no difference between the experiences of women and men who become parents biologically would not make sense. Women carry the babies, give birth to them, and have the capacity to continue to nourish them from their bodies, while men do not. But as Hays (1996: 14) points out, even though women have these capacities and may have "some animal-like instinct" to ensure their offspring's survival, "this makes up only a minuscule portion of what is understood as socially appropriate mothering." It's the meaning that's important, Hays notes — that these biological phenomena are linked to a particular ideology of mothering.

Meanings may be ascribed to biological differences that not only raise expectations for mothers, but lower them for fathers.

Belsky and Kelly (1994: 35–36) suggest, for example, that evolutionary programming could be responsible for fathers' lack of compulsion about helping with baby care: "When today's father says 'I can't stay and help; you know Dan and I always play racquetball on Saturday morning,' he may simply be displaying the most up-to-date manifestation of that ancient male impulse — limiting one's investment in the baby."

Even taking the "ancient male impulse" as biologically given, it is not necessarily clear that it leads to a father prioritizing a racquetball game over equity in his household. That is a socially constructed connection — an interpretation of biological difference. I would suggest that the father playing racquetball is doing gender, not biology. When biology is not interpreted as an obstacle to shared parenting, it isn't, as Renate Reimann (1997) found in lesbian couples in which one parent had a biological connection to the baby.

Two postpartum biological phenomena that the new parents I interviewed particularly imbued with social meaning were women's hormonal changes and their capacity to breast-feed. These were both equated with a uniquely female emotionality, although in different ways. While hormonal changes were used to rationalize responses to new motherhood that did not conform to good mother imagery, having the capacity to breast-feed was conflated with having the qualities of a good mother. In either case, the focus was on mothers', as opposed to fathers', capacity for giving care to infants.

Hormones and Mother-Infant Bonding

Some social scientists insist that there are gender differences between mothers and fathers that cannot be attributed to socialization alone (Rossi 1985; Udry 1994). They argue that women and men have different biological predispositions that shape their actions as mothers and fathers well before their first babies arrive, and that women's hormones, in particular, prime them for nurturing behavior.

The parents I interviewed, unlike these social scientists, did not conceptualize hormones as facilitators of maternal nurturance. In fact, those new mothers who mentioned hormones tended to do so in contexts that suggested their hormones interfered with their being happy mothers and wives. Hormones were perceived as the cause of negative experiences and of emotions such as depression and anger, and they were often used by mothers to explain feelings that they perceived as socially unacceptable.

Harriet, for example, talked about the "total turmoil" she felt during the first three days of her baby's life with the explanation, "I think your hormones are out of whack." Yet she went on to say that her mother-in-law had been visiting during these same three days. Lowering her voice so that her husband wouldn't hear, she told me that her mother-in-law drives her crazy. And it was pretty clear that her mother-in-law had this effect on her even when she hadn't just had a baby.

Laura said that she had been surprised by the hormonal changes she had experienced after giving birth: "I had a little bit of a depression. Not much. I had one day where I had like 'the blues,' they tell you. Pretty bad. But that went away." The qualifiers she used — "a little bit" and "not much" (despite the slip of "pretty bad") — reflect her discomfort with saying that she was depressed. Sociological study of postpartum illness reveals that serious depressions can be triggered in new mothers when they experience feelings that they believe conflict with how mothers are supposed to feel: anger, shame, anxiety, or disappointment. Verta Taylor (1996: 56) describes postpartum illness as a condition "tied to the white middle-class model of motherhood — that of a caring relationship almost entirely in women's hands."

When I asked Laura to tell me more about the source of her blues, she described a sense of not being sufficiently available to her baby as well as a sensitivity to how the nurses in the hospital were characterizing him. She said that on the day she had "the blues," she woke up in the hospital and heard her baby crying. As her statements reflect, she assumed that the crying was generated by her baby not being with her:

*He was in my room most of the time but when I needed rest
I would call the nurses, "Can you please get him out of here?
Just for an hour so I can take a nap." And I think he knew
where he was even as an infant, that he wasn't in the room
with his mother. And so I could hear him crying. So when
they would wheel him down the hallway, very often they'd
go, "Here comes Mr. Temper," and they would say things like
that. And sometimes it was funny, but that day nothing was
funny.*

Rather than labeling the nurses' comments as insensitive or in-appropriate, she attributed her own lack of a sense of humor to hormonal changes. Laura also used hormones to explain her bursts of anger about how much less Stuart's life had changed than hers: "I'll say to him, if I've had a hormonal week or some-thing, you know, 'I'm really feeling like cabin fever.' I'll say to him, 'You have no clue what this is like. Your life has not changed one iota.'"

Women described hormones as unsettling them rather than facilitating their mothering. Contrary to the image of a hormonal high wafting in to supplement the bliss of a new mother, Peggy perceived hormones as part of her less-than-ideal confrontation with new parenthood: "You think it is going to be all perfect, and you know, I knew everything about kids . . . It's still such a shock. You get home and you're like, what a handful at first. Especially at first cause that's when you're always tired, you know, you're run down. And that's when your emotions are going crazy and plus all of the hormone changes in your body."

Melissa is a twenty-eight-year-old white woman whose marital satisfaction had obviously been affected by the differentiation and unbalanced division of baby care between herself and her hus-band Brett. Rather than acknowledge any validity to Melissa's complaints, however, Brett attributed her unhappiness to hor-mones. He said that one day Melissa thinks their marriage has problems, and the next day she doesn't. He, on the other hand, didn't see them as having greater marital problems than they used to: "I don't know if I'm in a state of denial, but I don't think so . . . I think it's a hormonal thing. That may sound sexist, but I think that's it."

Melissa herself did not mention hormones; however, Brett reported that his mother had advised him to make sure that Melissa "doesn't go insane . . . that her hormones would be all screwed up." His assessment of Melissa's feelings about their marriage was that it was "cyclical" and "a hormonal thing."

To the extent that hormones were seen as responsible for anything in new mothers, they were not considered to be a positive influence. Instead, the comments reflected a perceived connection between hormones and depression, irrationality, and crankiness in women. A look at the index of the advice book most relied on by the women I interviewed reinforces this association of hormones with maladjustments to new motherhood. In *What to Expect the First Year* (Eisenberg, Murkoff, and Hathaway 1989), the subheadings under the listing "hormonal changes" are "postpartum depression" and "rejection of the breast." While the authors suggest that hormonal changes in new mothers may contribute to postpartum depression and make breast milk taste bad, it turns out that hormonal changes related to weaning from the breast can also trigger depression in mothers. According to this information, hormones can create depression both on the way into and out of breast-feeding.

The parents I spoke with interpreted hormones as a toxic force in what would otherwise be smooth transitions into motherhood. However, despite this dismissal of hormones as a facilitative influence on maternal nurturing, the question of whether there is an innately different bond between mothers and babies than between fathers and babies was taken seriously. Hormones were not identified as the source, but to many of the parents I interviewed, there seemed to be *something* biologically different about men's and women's relationships to their babies.

While some believed that fathers could have the same kinds of bonds with their children as mothers — if they spent the same amount of time with them — others believed that children were naturally more drawn to their mothers than to their fathers. Sylvia, for example, in speaking of "the mother-child bond," said that she wanted to believe that Sean could have the same kind of bond with their baby that she does, but she wasn't sure: "You just wonder physiologically I mean. I'm the one that gave birth . . . I mean I think they have a very intense bond too, but it doesn't, there certainly is a big difference. I'm sure that will change as Brian gets older, you know, he'll start to get involved with Dad more and have that period of being in touch with Dad. So I don't know. I just don't know."

Some fathers and mothers suggested that pregnancy shapes differences in the relationships babies have to their mothers. Since the baby grew in the mother's womb for nine months, it follows that they are closer:

> *She [wife] has said more than once that Dylan is closer to her in an emotional sense because they were together for nine months, you know, and I've got to believe that is true. (Jay)*

> *Everybody thinks that the man is supposed to make more money and then the wife stays home and takes care of the kids. And I can see why, because I'm so close to her, you know what I mean? I carried her for nine months; I had her. (Ashley)*

For some mothers, this construction may be a way of holding on to the special treatment that they got during pregnancy. Constance described pregnancy as a time when people are "courteous, kind, you wonder why can't people be like this all the time?" But they aren't once the baby arrives, as Peggy pointed out: "All of a sudden all of the attention that you used to get is shifted on the baby now and you're just kind of pushed to the side." During pregnancy, she said, "you have more of an excuse if you're tired . . . whatever you want to do then is really understandable." Once the baby arrives, she argued (I'm paraphrasing here): mothers become chopped liver.

Rhona Mahony (1995) suggests that pregnancy gives women a "head start" on attachment (although I have certainly met exceptions to this rule—women who found it hard to believe that they were really carrying babies and expressed various forms of amusement and annoyance about their husbands' conversations with their pregnant bellies). In any case, Mahony suggests that this advantage is accentuated by the usual practice of women staying home with the baby while men return to their jobs. She argues that if men spent more time alone with their babies early on, discrepancies between maternal and paternal attachment would disappear.[1]

Some of the new parents I met conflated notions of maternal "instinct" with having experience in taking care of babies. In talking about how her husband had not been around babies much, Whitney said that she didn't think that men have "motherly instinct." She then went on to say that nobody had ever shown Bob what to do if a baby was choking, and that he didn't know what their baby ate throughout the day: "When she was crawling especially, he would just kind of let her go and she would be picking things up and he'd be in the other room and not realizing things like that."

Whitney said that she would not trust Bob alone with their baby for a weekend. She would feel more comfortable leaving her baby with a female family member who had health training. My discussion with Whitney revealed that when given an opportunity to go away for a weekend, she had used the image of being a mother who did not want to separate from her baby as an excuse not to leave her baby with her husband: "I always said 'I don't want to leave her,' which was a little part of it, but I would have went . . . That would really, really hurt his feelings, I think, that I didn't trust him at that point to leave her."

While the concept of maternal instinct was treated like an explanatory variable by some mothers, it caused anxiety in others. Liza said that she had been concerned about her maternal instincts: "you know, that I wasn't going to have them." She had this concern because "I wasn't one of these women who was like, 'I can't wait to have a baby.'" Maddy told me in a recent follow-up interview that she had felt "maybe there's some sort of maternal things missing" in her. She went on to say that everyone she knew had seemed a certain way, but "then you wonder, is it really true, or have they learned that this is what the new mother does?" Maddy's comments imply a question about whether there is something instinctual about how new mothers "seem," or whether "the new mother" is a kind of social category that women interpret and "do."

Mandy talked about having revised her notion of maternal instinct based on seeing her husband's love for their child. She did not question the notion of instinct, but suggested that men could have it too: "I see how this baby has changed Chip's life and now I look at men who have children and say, 'Gosh, they must all love their children as much as Chip loves our baby.' And children really change a man and I don't think I really understood that before. . . . It's not just a motherly instinct. It is a parenting instinct I think."

While Mandy equated instinct with love, the concept of a unique mother-child bond often came up in discussions of caregiving as a kind of chicken-or-egg riddle. Which comes first: the division of labor or the child's preference for the mother? Whether it evolves naturally or is a function of time spent together, the mother-child bond was used to justify unequal divisions of baby care (and is probably reinforced by them since babies are likely to prefer the person who provides them with the most care).[2]

In discussing Sylvia as the primary caretaker, Sean saw their division of labor as both a function of their work schedules (hers part-time and his full-time) and of his agreement with Sylvia that their child has a stronger bond with her: "There seems to be a stronger bond between those two than there is between me and Brian. We're close but there seems to be a connection between the two of them that is stronger." When I asked him to what he attributed that bond, he replied, "I attribute it, I don't know if it's right or not, but I attribute it to her being motherly."

Even before Brian was born, however, Sean reported, "The

conversation I remember the most was her asking, 'Promise me you're going to help out with this kid.'" The assumption shared by Sean and Sylvia before the appearance of either their child or the bond was that Sylvia would be more involved and Sean would "help."

Following is an excerpt from an interview with a twenty-three-year-old, white, working-class woman who lived with her partner and their son. Both Maggie and Joel had responsibilities outside of their household. She worked in a clerical job and attended school part-time; he was a full-time tradesperson. Yet Maggie wondered why she seemed to take more responsibility for their son and why she didn't feel that she could go out as freely as Joel did. She articulated the question of the relationship between the notion of maternal instinct and societal norms: "I wish I knew why it was like that. Cause it doesn't have to be like that. If I wanted to just pick up and leave I could."

I asked her what kept her from leaving, and she explained, "I don't know. Maybe maternal instinct. Maybe there's a greater bond between child and mother than there is between child and father. Maybe that's just the way it is and it's always going to be like that . . . It seems like the mother's more connected to the child than the father. And I don't know if that's something that's just how we're born or if that's how society has made it."

"That's the big question," I said.

"That's what we have to get to the bottom of. . . . Or if it's something they can learn and be taught. So I don't know. But that's probably why I feel like I have more responsibility, you know. The bottom line, it comes down to me. Who's going to look out for things if I'm not here? And I think if I were just to pick up and say, 'Okay, see ya, I'm going out for the day,' I think he'd manage."

The questions that Maggie raises about the seeming relationship between a mother's greater biological connection to her children and her greater responsibility for them emerge in dynamics around feeding babies. Parents I interviewed whose babies were breast-fed often had more traditional divisions of labor than those that did not. Is this an inevitable outcome of breast-feeding? My answer is no (see also Reimann 1997), although I argue that fathers I spoke with became more involved when parents went against the advice of some baby care experts.[3]

PARENTAL ROLES AND FEEDING THE BABY

How babies will be fed gets attention unlike any other aspect of baby care. The very first question addressed in Chapter One of *What to Expect the First Year* is: "FEEDING YOUR BABY: Breast or Bottle?" This focus on feeding—which is a source of differentiation between mothers and fathers unlike other aspects of caring for and relating to a new baby—may have implications for how involved fathers are with their infants, since early involvement appears to increase fathers' confidence and commitment (Coltrane 1996). Feeding is also a source of differentiation among mothers themselves, and I will argue, based on interview data and an examination of breast-feeding literature, that advice about breast-feeding carries with it assumptions about how mothers should behave and feel in general.

Brendan suggested that fathers may react to the sense that they don't have the biological "goods" to nurture a baby by distancing from their children:

> *Contrary to what the woman's liberation movement may have been saying fifteen or twenty years ago, I think there's a difference between men and women, and that's wonderful. You know, there is a nurturing quality, and women do have breasts, and that's a biological thing, so there's a difference there. Men get disenfranchised there. They don't have that. There's some jealousy. So they kind of move away, isolate, build a wall, and I think it happens to all men. You can't, you know, it's like different. Women have always been known as the nurturing type. They take care, make sure that the daily type of things get done, you know? The socks get on, the school lunches get made.*

Implicit in Brendan's statements is the suggestion that men have a kind of "breast envy," which causes them to close off emotionally, leaving women to lead the field in caregiving, getting the socks on and the school lunches made. Brendan was not alone in making this association between breast-feeding and having particular nurturing qualities. Liza thought it was better to breast-feed than to bottle-feed but decided to bottle-feed because she didn't think she was "maternal." The leap between women having the capacity to breast-feed, and as Brendan put it, their being "known as the nurturing type," often appeared in couples' dynamics around feeding.

Of the twenty-five mothers I interviewed, seventeen breast-fed their babies: three for less than or approximately 3 months; five for 3+ to 6 months; seven for 6+ to 12 months; and two for more than a year. Four mothers began to breast-feed but quickly switched to bottle-feeding. And four mothers chose from the start to bottle-feed. For many of the parents I met, the decision about whether to breast- or bottle-feed was embedded in social relationships with friends and relatives as well as with the medical establishment.

As with other differences between mothers and fathers that appear to be given, women's capacity to breast-feed has not always generated the same responses in parents or in the people who advise them. Let me say a little about the historical context in which these parents were making decisions about feeding. The La Leche League, an organization formed to help nursing mothers, was founded in 1956. At that time, less than 10 percent of mothers were breast-feeding upon being discharged from the hospital with their new babies. Success in feeding formula to hospitalized sick infants had led many doctors to believe that bottle-feeding was just as good as breast-feeding. This was the environment encountered by the mothers of the women I interviewed, many of whom had given birth to their daughters sometime during the 1950s and early 1960s when mothers were being encouraged to bottle-feed. Breast-feeding eventually came back into favor with the medical establishment, and it became a governmental objective to raise the numbers of women breast-feeding their babies at the time of discharge from the hospital.[4] Consequently, the environment in which the women I interviewed became mothers was one in which they were encouraged to breast-feed.

While the medical establishment has swayed toward encouraging (and some new mothers argued, pressuring) women to breast-feed, many of the mothers (and mothers-in-law) of these women had been part of the bottle era and were not necessarily supportive of breast-feeding. Judgment from family members was apparent in Maggie's description of how Joel's family responded to her nursing: " 'Why are you nursing? Why not bottle-feed?' Duh duh duh duh duh. I just got flack the whole time. Nothing but resistance."

Barbara's comments convey the generational difference: "I think the nurses were very supportive. My mom, who was here and is a nurse wasn't that supportive, but she's not from that school. But she respected the decision that I made and I think my sister had gone through it and had sort of broken her into the idea. She just wasn't expecting me to be the kind who would breast-feed and I didn't think that I was going to be the kind either."

Barbara's comments illustrate the notion that a particular kind of mother breast-feeds. For Barbara, her sister's experience offset her mother's (and her own) resistance. Other women described their observations of sisters and friends as deterring them from breast-feeding:

My sister, for instance, nursed forever. And I think that's one of the reasons why I didn't. I mean her son was old enough to lift her blouse up and I just found that, it really, I'd just have to leave the room. (Sarah)

My sister, she tried . . . A lot of my girlfriends just had bad experiences with the baby not taking to them or just their breasts being so tender and cracked and bleeding and whatever they were. And I'm like, no, no thank you. I mean I'm not a martyr. (Liza)

While a few of the fathers said that they left the feeding decision up to their partner, many expressed a preference for breast-feeding. Some talked about the health benefits associated with breast-feeding as well as it being more natural. Arnie said, for example, "That's what God put them [breasts] there for, so why not use them?" Some fathers also mentioned the role of breast-feeding in facilitating a bond between a mother and child. For example, David said that it seemed "more of an intimate thing between the mother and the child": "I think I always wanted her to breast-feed . . . you sometimes hear things if you bottle-feed, you know, they won't be as close to the mother and this kind of stuff."

Interestingly, in Ehrensaft's (1990) study of parents who share parenting equally, many fathers who wanted a bond with their children as strong as their wives' expressed jealousy of their wives' capacity to breast-feed. At the same time, women in her study who were resisting doing gender in the form of having their whole identities wrapped up in mothering expressed ambivalence and resentment about having the full burden of breast-feeding.

The women I interviewed used their partners, family members, and peers as references in their decision making. But to the extent that new mothers felt pressure in relation to the decision, it tended to be generated by medical information about the benefits of breast-feeding. Andrea said, "I wasn't crazy about breast-feeding, but I ended up being convinced that when she's in fifth grade and fails a math test, it's going to be because I didn't breast-feed."

As the brief history above reflects, in the medical establishment the pendulum had swung from devaluing women's ability to nourish and provide immunity to their babies to what some mothers argued was guilt-tripping of mothers who chose not to breast-feed. Andrea commented on inconsistency in the messages:

> My sister-in-law, she breast-fed, and they talk about the immunities, but her son had chicken pox at three months and she breast-fed until he was nine months. So much for that.

> *I just kind of find it a mockery really when they breast-feed*
> *but then they're so quick to supplement. I'm like, now wait a*
> *minute here, breast milk is best, yet I have a friend who just*
> *had a baby the other day and she said, "Well my pediatri-*
> *cian said it's okay to supplement." Isn't this a riot? Breast*
> *milk is best, but it's okay, go ahead and use formula too. So*
> *ten years from now what're they going to say?*

Since the postpartum nurses encountered by new mothers spanned both their own and their mothers' generations, the support and advice they dispensed reflected the two different historical experiences. Some women described their appreciation for nurses who helped them learn to breast-feed while others appreciated nurses who let them off the hook emotionally if breast-feeding was not working for them. Still others, like Morgan, told stories of inconsistent advice and insensitive handling (literally): "The nurses were coming in and saying do this, do that and yanking on me [indicates her breast], try this, try that."

Gloria felt so pressured by the nurses to breast-feed — "pushing you, 'Why don't you want to breast-feed?' You know, you're committing a mortal sin" — that she told them she was going to bottle-feed. For her, having a nurse grab her breast and stick it in her baby's mouth was the final straw. Only after she had left the hospital and was home again did she resume breast-feeding.

Alison, who had planned on breast-feeding for six weeks before she returned to work, described her baby as not wanting to breast-feed. Her husband, Michael, also reported that their baby just wasn't "too interested in working too hard at it." The baby was becoming jaundiced, nurses were called in as well as a lactation consultant, and Alison said that she didn't know what to do: "Not that it bothered me that he didn't want to, but I just had two sides coming at me telling me what they thought I should do and how I should do it and I just had to be by myself and decide." When I asked her to describe the two sides, she said, "Basically the nurses who were saying, 'You don't have to breast-feed, just give him the bottle,' and then the lactation specialists . . . They just seemed pushier to me. So I just decided, put him on the bottle. I don't care. I wanted to do it for him, but I wanted him to also eat, and he wasn't interested in breast-feeding." Once the decision was made, she said that she felt fine, the baby was eating, and the jaundice went away.

There were other mothers who intended to breast-feed but switched to bottle-feeding. Constance said that everyone in her family had been bottle-fed, she saw nothing wrong with it, but she had tried breast-feeding: " Well I thought in terms of everything you read that it was best for him in terms of physical nurturing. But that was the only reason I wanted to. It didn't feel any maternal instinctive thing that I had to do this for whatever reason. And I am self-conscious about my body so I really didn't feel comfortable doing it so I was glad I couldn't."

"What does that mean that you couldn't?" I asked.

"Physically . . . Just couldn't do it. So that was great. And I was afraid that the lactation nurse there was going to try to convince me to do it, and she said, 'Hey, you don't want to do it, don't do it.' It really let me off the hook."

Andrea, who had ambivalently decided to try breast-feeding, described the following scenario after three days in the hospital: "They told me I had flat nipples." I asked her who had told her that, and she replied:

> *In the hospital . . . so they put me on an electric breast pump and I felt like a cow: pump, pump, pump. Then one of the nurses said there is a La Leche volunteer on the floor, let me have her come in, and in the meantime, they had been saying to try five minutes on each side, work your way up, toughen yourself, the whole bit. She came in, and I was trying to do the football hold and she told me I was doing it wrong. How can you hold a football wrong? You know what I mean? She said twenty minutes on each side. So I did, but I ended up bleeding. I was just a mess . . . So I tried it, I tried*

*it, but I wasn't all for it and once I went to the bottle, I was
just as happy as can be. And she was great and she loved it
and she has been really healthy.*

While these two mothers had not really wanted to breast-feed
in the first place, there were others who did, and for whom the
inconsistent advice threatened to sabotage something they really
wanted for themselves and their babies. One mother, Harriet, described how every nurse had a different idea about how to breast-
feed. One person said to wet the sleepy baby's face with a washcloth; another said to keep the baby's arms out of the way. Harriet
described herself as "to the point of total frustration": "I've got
these things [breasts], I've got this baby, and they're supposed to
work together, and they're not."

Once Harriet was home, her breasts so completely engorged
that she was unable to express milk from them, her husband,
Arnie, called a friend who was a lactation consultant. Harriet described the consultant walking in on the following scene. The
baby was wrapped tightly in a blanket because her arms "were
getting in my way": "Then we were wetting her face with a wet
washcloth until she screamed and then stuck her on the breast
and expected her to stick like glue."

The lactation consultant told Harriet to go have a drink, take
a shower, and then they would talk. When she returned, the consultant asked Harriet, "Would you like it if someone tied your
hands at your side, wet your face with a wet washcloth until you
were crying, and stuck your face in a plate of food?" The consultant sent Arnie out to get some formula and told Harriet, "You're
not a failure if you don't do this."

As it turned out, the consultant was able to show Harriet how
to breast-feed. This less-than-perfect initiation into breast-feeding
worked out well in the long run, Harriet said, because: "I breast-
fed and formula-fed and then when I went back to work the sitter
just gave her formula and I still breast-fed her like three or four
times a day." She felt good "being a working mom and breast-
feeding."

The model used by Harriet, combining breast-feeding and formula-feeding from the start, is not often used by mothers because they are concerned about sabotaging their breast-feeding, having been told not to introduce a bottle too soon:

> *I was scared. I didn't want to give her a bottle because once I got used to nursing, I'd hear all these stories about when you dry up or whatever. (Nancy)*

> *I think that you should be warned more, because I'm glad I did it for six months, but no one really warned me that at three o'clock in the morning for the first couple of weeks I'd be saying, oh why don't we just get a bottle . . . I just came so close so many times and the only thing that stopped me is having been told, if you stop, it's very difficult to go back or your milk supply will change and you are kind of sabotaging yourself. I didn't expect that I would want to stop that much. (Maddy)*

What happens in many cases, however, is unless a bottle is introduced relatively early, the baby turns it down later, as Ann Marie found out: "Because when you nurse they say don't give them a bottle for I forget how many weeks. So by then it's like he doesn't want a bottle."

The La Leche League emphasizes not introducing a bottle too soon, suggesting that babies become confused between breast and bottle nipples. While there were several stories in the group of parents I met of introducing bottles to their breast-fed babies quite early, the only tale of nipple confusion was from Miranda, who was clearly ambivalent about breast-feeding in the first place: "I breast-fed her for three weeks and she was such a pig. She was slobbering all the time, and so I gave her bottles to supplement and tried to wean her, and she got nipple confusion so I decided I'd just give her the bottle and she was fine." I asked her how she felt about making the change, and she said, "I was glad. It's very hard for me to get up every two hours of the night and then try to be in a good mood during the day. It was just easier for me to bottle-feed."

Again, let me remind readers that feeding is emphasized as one of the most important decisions that new parents make, and the rhetoric around breast-feeding is constructed in such a way that it appeals to mothers' "natural" desire to give their babies the best, while also suggesting that it is not always easy to get started. In other words, the advice that mothers get about breast-feeding is laden with the message that good mothers do it, but they won't necessarily be good at it. Therefore, mothers do not easily dismiss advice about how to make breast-feeding work, and the model Harriet used of combining formula- and breast-feeding was not the model the experts advise.

To the extent that the La Leche League acknowledges that a breast-feeding mother may find herself in the position of having to miss a feeding with her baby, they recommend that the mother pump breast milk: [5] "Mothers often ask about leaving a bottle of formula when they're gone, 'just in case.' We cannot recommend that you do that. Leaving your own milk assures you that your baby will continue to receive his favorite food. Does one bottle make that much difference? We wish we could say that it doesn't, but we can't. Even one bottle of formula can be a problem for some babies because of the risk of allergy" (La Leche League International 1987: 94).

Rather than suggesting that mothers (and fathers) try formula ahead of time to see if their babies are allergic, the La Leche League insists that mothers must use only their breast milk when they are absent from feedings. This trades a mother's constant presence for her constant preparation to be absent, and is, as some mothers described, an awkward project to accomplish while at work:

> *The only place to use the breast pump at work was in the*
> *restroom, which was not exactly the greatest place to go. It*
> *was not comfortable, and I never was able to get a whole lot*
> *with the breast pump. (Samantha)*

I'd be pumping in the truck, we worked out in the field, and it was ridiculous. Pumping in the truck. I mean that helped my supply to diminish. (Maggie)

The La Leche League's (1987: 94) guide to breast-feeding, *The Womanly Art of Breastfeeding*, merges advice about pumping breast milk with a particular message about how mothers are expected to feel. Following the passage quoted above is a section entitled "Alone is Lonely," which begins: "You won't want to leave your baby any more than you have to because babies need their mothers. It's a need that is as basic and intense as his need for food." In response to the notion that a mother has needs too: "But you may be surprised to find how strong the bond is that develops between you and your baby. A mother often finds that when she does leave her baby for that long awaited 'night out,' she worries so much about how the baby is getting along that she doesn't really enjoy the occasion!"

The message that babies need their mothers and their mothers' milk exclusively is one that caused several women I interviewed to feel that their feeding decision was a polarized one: either breast-feed or not; either be with the baby all the time or do not breast-feed. As Melissa said, "In the beginning I was going to just breast-feed until she was like seven or eight months, and I felt like I had a chain around my neck. And I was like, I can't do this all the time . . . I started supplementing and I felt like I was the worst mother in the world."

Melissa was comparing herself to her older sister who had breast-fed "straight" for eight months and "loved every moment." She said that she felt there was something wrong with her because she couldn't match her sister's behavior. On a visit to her doctor, she asked him if she was "a horrible person." The doctor relieved her anxiety, but her husband Brett was disappointed by the unexpected expense of having to buy formula: "He was like, 'That's going to cost money.' So I felt really guilty about that because when I had her I didn't go back to work and I was like, oh here's just another burden, so I felt really guilty about that."

As it turned out, Melissa nursed her daughter in the morning and at night for nine months and used a bottle during the day. She weaned Monica later than she expected to, and despite her initial belief that she had to breast-feed exclusively.

Unlike Melissa, employed mothers I met often had to confront the ideology attached to breast-feeding advice more directly because they were not always in a position to follow it. In a couple of cases, mothers decided not to breast-feed because they were going to be returning to work, but others did combine employment and breast-feeding and had to negotiate between their lifestyles and the advice of the experts. Ruth questioned the whole notion that breast-feeding is the optimal source of bonding between a mother and infant: "It was fine. I didn't find that like bonding thing that they talk about. I thought it was fine. It was nice, I didn't mind it, it was easy. I bonded with him just as much when I was holding the bottle as when I was nursing him. Actually I found that with the bottle, you can look at his eyes more because his face was up rather than into your chest."

Ruth and her husband introduced a bottle to their baby at six weeks in anticipation of her return to work at ten weeks. She breast-fed for three months, aware that she was going against the approach of the hospital where her baby was born: "They're very into breast-feeding. They would like you to breast-feed until your child goes to school if you could. I did it for three months. In three months he got all his antibodies, you know, and he started sleeping through the night."

Maddy, another mother who breast-fed for six months, said, "I think that it's given a whole mystique and maybe a lot of women find it this just beautiful wonderful experience, but I leaked."

Others truly enjoyed the unique connection they felt nursing their babies:

> *I loved nursing. I'd nurse him until college if I thought I could get away with it. (Eileen)*

> *It was something that I could give her that no one else could, and it was just a really tender moment. (Harriet)*

It is notable that the mothers quoted above, as well as the one that follows, were all employed full-time. In a nationally representative sample, Lindberg (1996) found that breast-feeding and employment seem to constrain one another: women are more likely to stop breast-feeding in the month that they enter employment. Also, women who work part-time are more apt to breast-feed, and to breast-feed for longer durations, than women employed full-time. Among the new mothers I met, however, there were women who negotiated their full-time jobs and breast-feeding. They were not conforming to the advice that they not leave their babies and may therefore have felt less constrained about other directives surrounding breast-feeding than Melissa, a stay-at-home mother who felt guilty about not nursing exclusively and having to spend money on formula.

Breast-feeding may also have been a particularly good antidote to any worries that employed mothers may have had about their relationships with their babies, as Samantha illustrates: "I came home for lunch every single day to feed her until I stopped breast-feeding. And she was the one who stopped it. . . . I was a little hurt when she decided that she didn't want to breast-feed anymore because it was really nice, and it was a really close feeling."

Aside from the issue of whether to supplement breast-feeding, some mothers and their partners expressed concern about whether they had breast-fed long enough. The La Leche League guide addresses weaning before one year as a kind of special issue, and *What to Expect the First Year* also implies that about a year is optimal, since it introduces a discussion of "thinking about weaning" in its chapter on the tenth month. Since most breast-feeding women do not continue beyond three to six months (Odent 1992), these guidelines may set women up to feel that they have not done enough. Maggie, who described herself as a promoter of breast-feeding, blamed herself for not living up to her expectation that she would nurse for a year:

It was real, it was, I mean I don't want to say it was hard for me. I'm sure a lot of people, but I had a crack, it bled con-

stantly, it hurt. But I made it four and a half months. And I was, that was probably the most heart-wrenching thing. I mean I was just determined to breast-feed until he was a year old. My first child, I wanted to nurse. I mean I'm really an advocate of breast-feeding. When somebody tells me they're bottle-feeding, I try not to let them know, but I'm kind of like [makes a disapproving face and laughs]. And that was really hard. I just started running out of milk.

A recent article in *Parenting* magazine reflects the message to mothers that they should wean later.[6] Despite the statement that 80 percent of American infants are fully weaned by the age of six months, the writers conclude a discussion of weaning "essentials" by discussing the weaning of a toddler: "A child responds best if his mother treats him with compassion, doesn't nag, and carries out her decision with resolve. Still, if weaning is making a toddler anxious, you may want to wait and try again in a few months" (Huggins and Ziedrich 1995: 122). The subtext of this passage is that a mother may initiate weaning out of her own, rather than her child's, interest and behave in a way that makes her child anxious. If this occurs, the mother should wait "a few months," the total length of time that most mothers breast-feed at all.

This article is followed by one entitled "Don't Rush Me," by a mother who is still nursing her three-year-old daughter. She makes an explicit connection between the fact that she herself was not breast-fed and that she turned out to be someone who "used the word *foreboding* to describe my attitude toward life." She blames her mother for not meeting her needs, and in particular, for not breast-feeding her: "Had she met my needs, had I been breastfed, maybe I would have been a Rhodes scholar, maybe I would be able to fly in an airplane without fearing it will fall out of the sky at any moment." She suggests that breast-feeding her daughter beyond infancy might help her daughter to have a "firmer footing" than the one her mother had provided her (Hey 1995: 124).

Feelings related to weaning were not only expressed by some

of the mothers I met, but by some of the fathers as well. David, whose wife did not particularly enjoy breast-feeding, said that he had been concerned that they had "kind of sped it up" when their baby was on a bottle by four or five months, having heard of other people breast-feeding through one year. Sean also expressed regret about his wife weaning their baby at eleven months: "When she started saying it was time to start weaning him, I said, 'Are you sure?'"

In contrast to the fathers above, two fathers whose partners had breast-fed for over one year expressed frustration with the impact they perceived breast-feeding to have had on their own bonds with their babies. In these two stories, the intersection of meanings imbued to feeding arrangements and a couples' general approach to parenting becomes apparent.

FEEDING AND RELATIONSHIPS BETWEEN BABIES AND PARENTS

Stuart described the pros and cons, from his perspective, of Laura's nursing their son:

> *It's nice at night, certainly nice at night. You get into a pattern where I don't even hear her sometimes. But on the other hand, you don't develop a certain, she's developed a certainly much closer bond to Nicky. I mean sometimes that's hard. I miss that. When he's cranky or whatever, there's only one thing that will satisfy him. And that's Laura and usually nursing. So that's kind of a bummer . . . I miss the relationship that might or may not have developed more with him. Because I never feed him.*

Stuart suggested that Laura doesn't necessarily allow him the opportunity to find another way to soothe Nicky. He described going into Nicky's room at night and Laura coming in after only a few minutes: "That's been a conflict at times because I think, how is he ever going to learn to settle down with me if he knows if he carries on long enough she's going to come in?"

Stuart went on to say that he could understand Laura's point of view — if she could come in and quiet the baby down, why not? He also said, however, that when Laura was not around, he and Nicky had no problems. But to the extent that Nicky doesn't like to be away from Laura, Stuart wondered how much it has to do with nursing: "I miss that part of the relationship that I see that she has because they're so much closer because of the nursing."

Elliot, whose partner had just weaned their baby at the age of eighteen months, also blamed nursing for his baby's lesser bond to him: "When our next child comes along what I would like to do is reduce the amount of time we breast-feed." I asked why, and he replied, "Just so I could feel more of a part of the feeding experience . . . I think that it's very important to breast-feed. I feel there's an incredible bond that's established between a mother and a child . . . I would have liked to have maybe bottle-fed at one point just so that it can be planted into our baby's brain that there's two parents. I sometimes feel, not a jealousy but just a frustration, when I can't get my daughter to understand, 'okay, mommy's left but dad's here,' you know, and everything's fine."

It is notable that both Stuart and Elliot attributed their less close relationships with their babies to breast-feeding. There were other possible explanations, such as the fact that they spent significantly less time with their babies than their partners did. It was also clear that in both cases they had not developed other mechanisms for soothing the baby besides nursing. In Reimann's (1997) study of lesbian couples' transitions into parenthood, she suggests that breast-feeding may be experienced as an obstacle to equal parenting in couples in which one mother is nursing and the other is not; some of the partners in her study also expressed frustration similar to that of Stuart and Elliot. However, Reimann notes, the effects of this biological difference were short-lived and rarely resulted in long-term differentiation in roles. More important than biological connection was ideological commitment to equality. In other words, the couples she interviewed did not see breast-feeding as a major and lasting barrier to people who believed in coparenting and wanted to do it.

Cowan and Cowan (1992: 103–104) refer to couples' interactions around breast-feeding as an example of a "marital dance" in which men feel pushed out of caretaking by women.[7] Yet they also acknowledge that many nurses and doctors "emphasize breast-feeding almost exclusively" and "may not mention or actively frown upon the use of supplemental bottles." As we have seen, mothers tend to take responsibility for seeking out and interpreting information; their marriages may then be stressed when they try to act on their interpretation of this advice. Coltrane (1996) describes arguments between mothers and fathers in his study of couples who share parenting about whether to supplement breast-feeding with formula; fathers were more likely to argue for supplementing. Perhaps mothers in Coltrane's study were trying to push fathers out, but they may also have been struggling with the apparent conflict between including their husbands and doing what they had surmised from experts is better for babies, which is not to supplement.

If Cowan and Cowan (1992) heard about how Laura and Stuart negotiate Nicky's nighttime waking, they might interpret Laura as pushing Stuart out of caring for Nicky; on some level, this was how Stuart interpreted Laura's behavior. I want to suggest, however, that there are other ways to perceive her behavior. Laura was a mother who described herself as worrying that her child was feeling abandoned any time she heard him crying in his crib. If Stuart did not take responsibility for saying in the middle of the night, "Let me try; we'll be okay," it is difficult to imagine that a mother immersed in baby care and breast-feeding advice (as Laura was) would independently push that solution onto him. It is important to recognize that there may be mothers who would welcome their husbands' participation in feeding if it did not appear to be against expert advice that reinforces worry about what happens when mothers are not available to their babies.

I do not mean to suggest that mothers are simply passive recipients of expert advice who just do whatever people tell them to do. In fact, some of the mothers I've described in this chapter illustrate that mothers are active evaluators of advice and do not necessarily conform to it. Rather, I suggest that for a mother to integrate a father into a context in which she believes that *she* should be available requires action on her husband's part — a willingness to find his own way to soothe the baby and reassure his wife about going against her parental consciousness. And, as LaRossa (1997) points out, cultural prescriptions intersect with political interests. Advice to mothers does not invite them to include fathers, and fathers may (unconsciously or not) be served by this advice.

In both of the cases I presented above, it was not just the fathers who were ambivalent about how long the mothers nursed; the mothers themselves were too. Laura, who was still nursing thirteen-month-old Nicky at the time of our interview, had planned to wean him at one year: "I'm going to try to feel him out about it. I always thought I would stop at his first birthday or when he got teeth. I always thought that, but it seems like his relationship with me, part of it is defined by us nursing together, and I think that at some point that is going to have to change and I don't know when that occurs, I'm just kind of taking cues from him."

She went on to say that Nicky was fine about drinking and going to sleep with other people through processes other than nursing, but that he defines her as "you're the person I nurse with." Laura expressed worry about being a certain type of mother with a certain type of nursing child: "I don't want to be the mom that nurses her child, I don't want him to ask for it or be out in public and have him pull my shirt up. I don't want to go to kindergarten to give him his morning milk. So I definitely want to put a limit on this at some point. So I don't know. I know we have plans to have another baby at some point. Maybe that'll help. It's sister's turn. [Laughs]."

The effects of nursing too long were also a worry for Elliot's partner, Nancy, who had just weaned their eighteen-month-old child: "I was beginning to worry about that like towards the end when I'm nursing her this long, she's gonna be like this mama's girl. Like she'll tell on her friends to me and I call the principal. I don't want it to be like that."

It is interesting that the two mothers who conformed to the advice provided by the experts worried about whether their children would be *too* bonded to them. For these mothers and their partners, breast-feeding was perceived as potent, and on some level, treacherous bonding that had a great impact on how involved they thought a father could be when the mother was present.

Within male-female couples, breast-feeding could be a hook on which a father who did less than his share of baby care could hang his hat. Ted—who had begun the interview confessing that he thought he should do more with the baby—said, when I asked at the end whether there was anything we hadn't covered, "You didn't ask me if I get up in the middle of the night, which I don't. . . . It's a good thing he doesn't depend on me to survive because I've never even heard him. He never wakes me up. I sleep right through it and she wakes up when he makes a peep."

"Is that why you don't get up?" I asked.

"It probably would have been different if I knew he was depending on me," he replied.

Brendan said, "At night I'm very happy . . . I wasn't going to say, 'Pump your breasts and I'll feed him.' I've got to go to work the next day. So it's very easy to get into that division of labor." I asked him if he would have gotten up at night if they had been bottle-feeding; he answered, "Not if she wanted to."

Melissa talked about how Brett never got up with their baby, Monica, at night: "At night he never got up with her because she breast-fed. And that was hard. That's still a touchy subject. I'm like, there's no reason why even if she has that little bottle at night, but his reasoning is he has to go to work."

Brett said that this was the way their baby wanted it, although he implicitly suggested that if his behavior had been different, Monica might have wanted something different: "She [Melissa] had to do all the work. I don't want to be a male chauvinist and say that was her job, but that's what Monica wanted and I don't know if it was because she just didn't get the attention from me or what. So Melissa did all the work."

In contrast are the comments of Wade, whose wife switched from breast- to bottle-feeding: "Andrea tried breast-feeding but she wasn't real keen on it. She just thought she owed it to the baby to give it a try because people would say, 'Well she tried, it's better,' blah, blah, blah, and the whole deal, but it depends on who you talk to too. Some people say it doesn't really matter." Wade went on to say that he had wanted to be a part of the feedings and did not see why Andrea should bear the brunt of getting up at night: "I was happy to get up in the middle of the night and give the baby a bottle. It didn't bother me at all."

Exclusive bottle-feeding provided an obvious opportunity for fathers to share feeding responsibilities, as Ashley described: "I stayed up late with her and then he'd get up at like four o'clock with her and then when he got up for work he'd usually give her a bottle and put her back to bed so I could sleep."

Yet it was also possible for fathers to be involved even when babies were breast-fed. Jake's use of "we" in describing the way he and his wife approached feeding is notable: "He was always supplemented so we kind of had like a system where I usually stayed up later so when we started to wean him off to a bottle and supplement, I did the late feedings and she did the early mornings, or the middle of the night."

Using a bottle exclusively was also no guarantee that, as with other "shared" aspects of baby care, mothers wouldn't ultimately have more responsibility, as Sarah illustrates: "As far as making the bottles, I did most of that, although Eddie is getting better at it now that we're almost finished with bottles. But he doesn't feel like he did it right." When I asked, "Did you think he did it right?" Sarah replied, " At first he used to crank the covers on so tight that it ripped the bag, so we did have to have a talk about that [laughing]. He said, 'Well you do it then,' so I did it for a long time. But now he realizes."

Jack said of his and his wife's division of labor: "The only thing

I think that she does totally is pack his lunch. That's something that I'm not familiar with, but I've done it on occasion and it went fine . . . It was hard in the beginning working with bottles. That was something I never cared for much." Not caring much for working with bottles had extended into an unfamiliarity with making lunch.

Still, in cases where mothers were breast-feeding, the caregiving function was often perceived as literally attached to them. Ann Marie described nursing as setting up a routine in which she took over the feeding duties even when it came time for a bottle or food. Peggy generalized nursing to caregiving in general: "I breast-fed in the beginning so even though he helped me as much as he could I was still the constant caregiver."

Although there are many other kinds of care that babies need besides feeding as well as ways that breast-feeding can involve fathers (fetching, holding, burping, and so forth; see Parke 1981), breast-feeding frequently served to differentiate mothers from fathers. To paraphrase Brendan, mothers have breasts and fathers don't; mothers therefore have a capacity to take care of babies that fathers don't. This was a message that came through in expert literature about breast-feeding, and it was acted out in interactions between new mothers and fathers.

The notion that there is a lot riding on feeding decisions is evident in a doctor's foreword to the La Leche League guide to breast-feeding. Describing the scientific corroboration of what "nursing mothers did by natural inclination and intuition," Dr. Herbert Ratner writes of the "maternal attachment phenomenon": "Only now are we beginning to grasp the extent to which the undermining of the maternal attachment process with its reciprocal bonding of infant to mother has contributed to the maternal and adult delinquency of a sick society." The reward of the "renascence of breastfeeding," Ratner writes (La Leche League International 1987: xviii-xix), is: "Mothers and infants will become bosom friends, and society will reap the benefits."

It is my contention that information about breast-feeding dispensed by medical personnel and other breast-feeding experts may merge into ideology about the maternal role (and indirectly reinforce a view of fathers as peripheral to babies' care). There are clear benefits to babies being breast-fed, and I know from my own experience how meaningful it can be to breast-feed, but advice that is given to facilitate breast-feeding often results in stress and guilt for mothers who either feel that they cannot get a break, or that if they do, they are not doing enough. The emphasis on breast-feeding to the exclusion of other forms of nurturing, soothing, and caregiving, elevates mothers' primacy to their babies in ways that may affect fathers' involvement with their babies.

What is the relationship between the discussion of hormones with which this chapter began and the discussion of breast-feeding with which it ends? In both cases, the meanings ascribed to these biological characteristics that are supposed to predispose mothers to caregiving ultimately devalue mothers. Hormones are discussed by fathers and mothers in ways that reinforce a sense of female, chemically-driven irrationality. Using hormones as an explanation for mothers' negative feelings may also mask problems that are not necessarily determined biologically.

Breast-feeding is also approached by those promoting it in a way that does not truly take mothers' needs into account. Rather, as Barbara Katz Rothman (1989) has argued about the making of babies in general, mothers are treated (both in how their "parts" are handled and in the rhetoric surrounding breast-feeding) as vehicles for the production of quality infants. Mothers' commitment, sacrifice, and dedication to their babies is minimized. Both mothers and fathers are done a disservice by the use of breast-feeding to promote a particular image of mothers.

Whether biological differences do in fact determine differences in parenting, it is clear that they may be interpreted in ways that justify gendered divisions of baby care — or not. Fathers may not be able to breast-feed, but they *can* be very involved with breast-fed babies if breast-feeding is not conceptualized as an obstacle to father involvement. One physiologist, Jared Diamond, argues that men actually have the physical capacity — nipples and mammary glands — to nurse:

> *Research has shown that men who undergo hormone treat-*
> *ments for cancer occasionally secrete breast milk; some tran-*
> *quilizers can stimulate milk production in men; and males*
> *who suffer from starvation have been known to lactate . . .*
> *Emerging social trends could unlock all men's ability to*
> *nurse. The rise in multiple births linked to fertility drugs, for*
> *example, could eventually create a demand for new sources*
> *of parental nourishment. (That means you, Pops.)*
> *So does this mean that men will soon be pumping breast*
> *milk between business meetings? Not so fast. At least one*
> *major hurdle remains, Diamond says: "Men may have a*
> *hard time getting used to the idea that breastfeeding isn't*
> *just a job for women" (Gluck 1995: 24).*

There is a jump between seeing breast-feeding as a job for women and constructing all forms of caring for a baby as "women's work." For some new parents, breast-feeding was used as a rationalization of little involvement from fathers, and for others it was not.

As much research as there is suggesting that differences in men's and women's approaches to parenting are biologically based, there is also research refuting this notion.[8] Even the assumption that mothers are more sensitive and responsive to infant cues in the context of feeding has been contested (see Parke 1981). But whether or not mothers are innately better at parenting than fathers is a different question from whether fathers can do it at all; as William Marsiglio (1993: 490) notes, most scholars agree that "men are not inherently deficient in their ability to parent." Yet the institutional script that new parents get reinforces an image of biological difference as a formidable determinant of parenting arrangements; so it is with each other that new mothers and fathers can either reproduce or rewrite the dialogue.

❦

CHAPTER 5

As a Wife and a Mother: Marriage and Approaches to New Parenthood

RUTH TALKED ABOUT WHAT IT MEANS TO HER TO be "the wife and mother" by saying that she responds more quickly to their crying baby than her husband does. We've explored some of the connections between being a mother and responding to a baby — but what does being a wife have to do with it? In this chapter, I argue that dynamics between parents are shaped in part by dynamics in marriages. Seems to make sense, right? But to the extent that this has been recognized in research literature, wives have been seen as influencing and even imposing barriers to their husbands' involvement with babies (see Belsky and Volling 1987; Berman and Pedersen 1987, Cowan and Cowan 1987), while the factors shaping mothers' involvement — including their husbands — have not necessarily been examined. This imbalance implicitly suggests that women's responses to becoming mothers are fixed while men's responses are shaped by their wives.

But from the "doing gender" perspective, there is no "wifing" without "husbanding." In other words, wives do not create child care arrangements alone; they and their husbands do it together, and they do it in the context of a relationship arrangement that, like parenthood, has been institutionalized: marriage. In this chapter, I argue that the existence of gender differentiation in new parenthood is reinforced by gender hierarchy that is already embedded in men's and women's relationships with each other and in the institution of marriage. Before elaborating this point, however, I discuss one way that new parenthood affects marriages. That is the role that gender differences in parental consciousness play in decreases in marital satisfaction.

PARENTAL CONSCIOUSNESS AND COUPLE INTERACTIONS: EFFECTS OF THE WHO-HAS-IT-WORSE? SYNDROME

There's a "Cathy" cartoon (Guisewite 1995) in which a child tells her mother that she doesn't want her to go to work. The mother responds, "Oh baby, I'm so sorry," then thinks to herself, "Why am I working?? Do I *have* to work? Could we possibly make it if I *didn't* work? Will I always regret this time working? Is there any way I could work *less*? Do I have to work?? *Why am I working? Why? Why?*" The child then says to her father that she doesn't want him to go to work. His response: "Don't be silly, honey. Of course I'm going to work." No apology, no second thoughts. The mother thinks to herself, "Is there anything more annoying than witnessing inner peace?" [1]

This mother's annoyance with her husband's inner peace and her lack of it is a factor in marital conflict that often emerges with the transition to parenthood. Although new parenthood does not necessarily exert any one consistent effect on marital relationships (Belsky and Rovine 1990), the tendency toward greater gender differentiation has been associated with decreases in marital satisfaction (Belsky, Lang, and Huston 1986; Cowan et al. 1985; Ruble et al. 1988). Wives are particularly prone to experiencing a decline in satisfaction with their marriages following the birth of a first child (Cowan and Cowan 1988b; Harriman 1985; Miller and Sollie 1980; Waldron and Routh 1981). It may be that women's disappointment in their partners stems not only from unequal divisions of physical labor, but from their loneliness with the mental experiences they have as new mothers.

Miranda, for example, is a twenty-one-year-old, white, working-class military wife attending school part-time and pregnant with a second unplanned child. She did not question her primary responsibility for baby care, but complained that her husband Gil didn't help when their child was "throwing a fit": "I mean he's just a guy. I don't think it clicks sometimes." Not only was Miranda frustrated by the implications of things not "clicking" for Gil in terms of getting concrete help from him, but she also described an absence of emotional support because of what Gil does not know about what goes on in her head [emphases added]:

> *It really hurts, because he doesn't know how high my intentions or whatever or goals for being a good mom are . . . [crying].* He doesn't know what I think *and when he's at work he doesn't know when she starts screaming and throwing fits, or pulling everything out of the dishwasher when I'm trying to load it,* and I've got all this in the back of my head *that I have to do for school, and the house is a mess, and supper's not cooked and he'll be home in thirty minutes.* He doesn't know that I have to keep telling myself, "Be calm. Love your child." *You know? He doesn't know. So I just get upset when sometimes I really think he would say, "Well she could be a better mom."* But he doesn't know.

After making this complaint, Miranda suggested that perhaps she was asking too much of Gil: "I guess I expect him to read my mind. And he can't. And he doesn't stress out if the house isn't spotless, and I do. So how can he read my mind? He's not like me."

Miranda's statement that Gil does not "stress out" like she does masks that she is held responsible for housework. It was especially poignant in light of the fact that, earlier in the interview, she had described Gil cleaning the house that day and commenting to her that it was the cleanest it had been in a long time and that she "never do[es] anything." It is the invisibility of what new mothers do, and especially of what they think, that can create conflictual interactions between new parents.

In a journal about her first year as a single mother, Anne Lamott (1993: 150) describes a conversation she had with a friend about whether having a husband makes having an infant easier:

> She said, "Oh, no, just the opposite. The only real advantage is that you get to have tantrums and someone to attack, which, actually, the more I think about it, does seem to relieve some of the pressure. You get to say things like 'I hate my life, I hate you, you're gone all day, this was your idea, my figure is ruined, you're a bad person, I hate you, and I hate listening to you floss every night. It makes me want to hang myself.'"

This anecdote conveys the pressure that differences in women's and men's experiences of new parenthood can put on their marriages. Among the new parents that I interviewed, differences in parental consciousness created marital stress in both concrete and symbolic ways. Concretely, women got less help from their husbands than they expected or were unhappy with having to ask for help, and this created conflict. Symbolically, new mothers spoke to resenting their husband's freedom and feeling a lack of recognition of their own sacrifices from their husbands. In some cases, fathers functioned as a kind of mouthpiece for expectations of them as mothers: generating guilt in them about their mothering and reinforcing the sense that they were ultimately responsible for their babies.

Morgan and Ken are both thirty-three years old, white, and middle class, and are full-time employees of the same company. Ken had a higher position than Morgan that allowed him more control of his hours, but Morgan felt guilty asking Ken to pick their child up at the baby-sitter: "When I really need him to pick her up from the baby-sitter he will, but I drop her off every morning and I pick her up probably four nights a week out of five and I'm always feeling guilty. Even if he picks her up one night a week, I feel guilty about it. I don't know if it's me or if it's him making me feel guilty or what."

Ken said the following about Morgan being late to pick their child up at the baby-sitter: "I think it's pretty rude to do that to the baby-sitter myself. I would never do it. I'd leave. There's nothing that would keep me here [workplace] if I had to go." What Ken described as a trend, Morgan presented as an isolated event that occurred when Ken was out of town for work. She talked about how "awful" she felt about being late to the baby-sitter. Although the baby-sitter did not have a problem with it, Morgan said, "I just hate doing that, I just felt so guilty."

Ken said that he puts his home life before work and that Morgan is "the exact opposite." He questioned Morgan's priorities, while she saw their division of labor as the conflict: "This is an ongoing argument that we have. Ken helps out a lot but there's things that I wish he would do more of—like he hardly ever changes her diaper." Although Morgan described herself as feeling "awful" and "guilty" about aspects of her mothering, if Ken was aware of her feelings, he did not help her to take herself off the hook emotionally; rather, he suggested that Morgan should be doing more than she was.

Whitney and Bob are an example of a couple whose marriage was stressed by Whitney's perception that Bob did not recognize the greater sacrifices she had made. Both white and from working-class backgrounds, twenty-eight-year-old Whitney had left a job in banking following the birth of their baby, while Bob, twenty-six, continued his work as an engineer in the military. In a refrain from what was apparently a chronic disagreement about "who has it worse," Whitney said: "Well we always discuss this, we always have different opinions. I feel it was a bigger change for me only because I gave up everything. I mean, I worked full-time and I completely gave up my job. I gave up all the security that I had with that, all the benefits that my job gave me."

She expressed the feeling that with all that she had given up,

Bob should give up something too: "I mean he used to be able to just go with the guys whenever, wherever, and it was never a problem with me . . . I think that was a big change for him because he still wanted to go out and do the things that he used to. It's like I can't even go to work anymore, you know? You have to give up some of your privileges that you had."

She went on to tell me that she really had given up more than Bob, although it was something they debated all the time: "It's like raising kids or raising a child, it is work. Staying home all day with her is my work, no matter how rewarding it may be, you're still up at 7:00 in the morning."

I asked her if there were any disputes about that, and Whitney replied, "All the time. All the time. . . . That gets nasty sometimes. It does, it gets nasty sometimes. He really doesn't understand. He's never really been home twenty-four hours a day, every day, seven days a week with her like I have."

Having what Larson has referred to as a "climate of attunement" is a key factor in marital quality across the transition to parenthood (Mason and Perry-Jenkins 1997). Couples I met who were in conflict about who had it worse had trouble empathizing with each other's losses. For mothers, losing their autonomy, earnings, and their bodies as they had known them seemed much greater than the loss of activities that fathers tended to invoke. One of the ways that some husbands indirectly invalidated their wives was by suggesting that the constraints women felt as a result of becoming mothers were not real, or by saying "I would stay home in a minute," when there was actually little chance of it. Invariably, a husband's offer to cover for his wife came in the middle of an argument, as Stuart described: "I've said lots of times, 'Just do it and Nicky and I will be fine.'" I asked what Laura says, and he responded: "It's either in an argument and she'll say, 'Okay, I'll do it then!' Or I don't know, she just feels it isn't practical."

Whether Laura had to be as compulsively present as she felt she did was a question that she did not ask in the context of feeling that she was the one with whom the buck stopped. In other words, the content of her parental consciousness was a sense of pervasive and ultimate responsibility. It was also difficult for Stuart to acknowledge that Laura's approach evolved, at least in part, because of his own lack of mental labor and physical availability. Stuart talked instead about it being Laura's personal "philosophy" to be with their child.

Another pressure placed on their marriage was that Laura's greater sense of responsibility kept her from seeing women friends from whom she might receive emotional support. Laura said of how this affected her relationship with Stuart: "I need him sometimes to be my girlfriend and he's not . . . I didn't realize how much more I need him to be sensitive now that I don't have more women involved in my life. I think that's the big thing. I feel sorry for him because he wasn't ready for that [laughs]. He wasn't ready to fill this void and I think it's kind of unfair to him. You don't realize how much you need those other people until you see them less frequently."

Munch et al. (1997), who document decreases in women's social networks after having children, suggest that the restriction of mothers' social worlds could have implications not only for how much social support they receive, but also for their access to information and job sources. Mothers' sense of physical accountability to babies may lead them to cut off from other women, as Laura did, and cultural imagery of marriage and parenthood as private partnerships between women and men may obscure this loss (McMahon 1995; Rich 1976).

Of the mothers I spoke with, Melissa was one of the most open about how out of control her life felt during her baby's first year and how the expectation that she should be in control was affecting her marital satisfaction. Melissa's baby, Monica, was very small when she was born, and Melissa described herself as quite apprehensive with her, "a wreck," "like I just didn't know where one day was going." Melissa said that she was "scared" of Monica: "I didn't feel comfortable with her. She wasn't colicky but she was just hard to handle when she was little . . . nothing could content her."

While Melissa experienced Monica as inconsolable at times, her husband, Brett, described Monica in her first few months as "a leech, a mama's girl." Brett's use of the term "mama's girl" suggests another underlying dynamic in the who-has-it-worse syndrome: men's envy of their babies' attachments to their wives and their sense of rejection when they feel unable to soothe their babies. In different ways, both Brett and Melissa perceived Melissa as the primary parent of Monica, yet often even Melissa could not soothe her: "There were nights when she would just be up for like three or four hours, and I'd feel so guilty, but we'd put the swing in the bedroom and put her in there and we'd wake up in the morning, and I was like the worst mother." (Notice Melissa's use of pronouns: "we" put her in the swing, but "I" was "the worst mother.")

When Melissa was unable to "control" Monica, she described herself as lashing out at Brett: "I took it out on Brett. I mean whenever I didn't have control, like I couldn't comfort her, it was like, 'You don't help me.' And I'm still like that sometimes, I'm like, 'You have to help me — not just sit there and watch her want me.'"

Melissa described her fears about her marriage: "You just keep hoping that one day it'll all get back in control and there're some days I think that this just isn't working out, and it's frightening because we have her [baby], you know? And we're a unit and you have to fight it sometimes, but you're like it would be so much easier just to say forget it."

I asked her if she was referring to her relationship with Brett, and she replied, "Yeah. And it's just like you go in spurts where everything seems to be, he seems to be doing fifty-fifty, and then other times, when I can't keep doing this, I'm going to burn myself out plus make everyone else miserable. I mean, we talk about it, you know, it gets to the point where we just have to sit down and talk about it, but you wish you didn't have to talk about it, it would just come naturally."

Melissa was frustrated that she had to ask Brett to do his share, yet she also felt that she should spare him from her frustration.

She would question herself after she expressed her feelings: "I mean he hears it all day [at work] and then to come home and there's times when I know I should bite my tongue and I don't."

The counterpart of Melissa feeling underappreciated and wanting more help was Brett feeling nagged. Although he told me that his vision for his family was that they would take a lot of vacations, he said that he did not want to take one currently: "I don't think there's a return on the investment because what am I going to do? Take Monica to Florida and sit on the beach and listen to Melissa scream about how she's got to watch her and I'm not paying any attention to her?" Brett knew what was making Melissa upset and angry, but he did not feel that their marriage was in trouble; rather, as I mentioned in Chapter 4, he chalked Melissa's unhappiness up to hormones.

These stories are consistent with the association established in past research between increased gender differentiation and low-ered marital satisfaction (for women in particular). Yet there were stories from other new parents suggesting that when women felt emotionally supported by their husbands, not only did they not appear to resent their differences, they did not even acknowledge them. In some couples, there was a surprising lack of admission of difference, even in cases in which one partner (in all but one case a woman) had clearly experienced greater change in the transition to parenthood. Several women even argued that their husbands had experienced more change, despite evidence to the contrary.

Maddy had left a job to be home with her baby full-time and suggested that it might be easier to be the primary caregiver "be-cause then you're totally immersed in this and you sort of expect the changes." She thought it was harder for her husband, who has to "change gears" when he comes home from work and doesn't get to establish a rhythm "twenty-four hours a day."

Mandy had also left a job to stay at home full-time. She said of the changes she and her husband had experienced: "I think that it has been the same. I think that we are both surprised at how much you can completely and utterly just love the baby." At the same time, Mandy said that her husband was "the first one that tells me how hard of a job it is." Rather than arguing that he had it worse, Chip acknowledged the work in Mandy's caring for their baby as well as his "luck" in not being the one to stay home with him: "I kind of lucked out because I make more."

Later I will argue that these arrangements have consequences for women's power base in their marriages, as well as for their future economic stability, but in the short-term, these couples were not fighting over who had it worse. Since I met these new parents at only one point in time, I don't know whether some couples were simply happier than others in their marriages prior to becoming parents, although I suspect that this is not a full explanation. In some cases, I think that the women were relieved to be home after leaving dissatisfying employment. But I would also argue that a couple's explicit understanding that parenting is work—mental as well as physical—made a difference in how supported women felt by their husbands.

Another explanation, however, may be that these women did not see their gender differentiation as unfair because they experienced themselves as wanting it. Marjorie DeVault (1991: 161) suggests that women's accommodations to husbands and children are often experienced by them as choices they are making, and because of this, they may "come to define deference as equity."

GENDER HIERARCHY IN MARRIAGE AND NEW PARENTHOOD

I want to suggest that the increased gender differentiation that occurs with new parenthood may be conceptualized, at least in part, as fitting into patterns already established in husbands' and wives' relationships. Though talked about as equal partnerships, marriages often contain dynamics of inequality and accommodations of men by women that are embedded in heterosexual marriage as an institution (DeVault 1991; Komter 1989; Johnson 1988; O'Connor 1991).

The legal traditions that shaped marriage as an institution in the past are embedded with gender hierarchy, as Scott Coltrane (1996: 38–40) notes: "In past times, women gave up legal rights when they married, and acquired a set of obligations that tended to be rather severe . . . the husband and wife became a unity upon marrying, and that unity was the husband." He identifies the following four provisions that were incorporated into statutes governing marital contracts in the United States:

1. *The husband is the head and master of the household*
2. *The husband is responsible for financial support*
3. *The wife is responsible for domestic services*
4. *The wife is responsible for bearing and raising children*

Was that then, and this is now? Clearly, like dominant imagery of parenthood, norms surrounding marriage are negotiated in a variety of ways by women and men "doing" marriage. Yet while both the fathers and mothers that I interviewed were well aware of gendered expectations for new parents, there were differences in their perceptions of the impact of gender on marriage when no children were involved. Fathers were less apt than mothers to identify differences in societal expectations for husbands and wives, but there were a few:

> *The husband is usually the person that goes out into the job market and brings home the bacon, so to speak, and the woman is the one who fries it up in the pan. (Jay)*

> *I think that society has different expectations for men than for women so a lot of differences between husbands and wives are just extensions of that. Women are expected to be supportive and nurturing and men are supposed to be take charge and less emotional. (Phil)*

More often, even fathers who characterized themselves as relatively traditional talked about marriage now being a shared enterprise:

Today you kind of have to work together to create a future.
(Bill)

You remove the kid and I don't think these roles of caretaker
and provider apply. (Arnie)

Husbands versus wives, expectations? Boy, offhand, no . . .
I think in today's society . . . it's outdated. They're both
equal. (Chad)

Despite many husbands' perceptions that marital roles were
no longer differentiated, there were vestiges of gender hierarchy
in their discussions. Chip, for example, said about what it means
to be a good wife: "I think a good wife is somebody who's committed to marriage, but retains her individuality — committed to
a marriage to a point where she is not sacrificing her own self."
When he spoke about what good husbands do, it was to allow
wives to express themselves: " I think a good husband, again, is
committed to the marriage and allows his wife to express herself
as well as himself, and not put himself ahead."

Chad talked about couples doing "whatever works," yet in
talking about himself, he stressed his greater physical capability
as well as his being able to "pawn off" on his wife things that he
chooses not to do: "Whatever works to get the job done or whatever works to make ends meet or whatever works to make it happen. You know, you take the strengths of both, the weaknesses of
both, or what you like doing and what you don't like doing and
you try to compromise. Easier said than done."

"To compromise?" I asked.

"Yeah, or to find that balance. Checkbook writing, balancing
the checkbook, chores, certain things I do that I enjoy, certain
things I do because I am more physically capable of doing them.
What I don't like doing I try to pawn off on Constance. Hopefully
she doesn't mind doing them."

DeVault (1991) suggests that gender dynamics are often masked
by an emphasis on "practicality." Some of the husbands I inter-

viewed benefited from the fact that it was "practical" for their wives to take more responsibility for their babies without having to acknowledge the lack of egalitarianism between them that was generating this state of affairs.

National surveys reveal that married men are more likely than other men to hold traditional attitudes, particularly about bread-winning responsibilities. Citing other research as well as her own, Jane Riblett Wilkie (1993: 277) comments that the persistence of traditional ideology may reflect "resistance to the loss of bread-winner status and the privileges in the home to which being the breadwinner has entitled them . . . Married men as a group lose more than single men from women's employment in terms of di-minished personal services from wives and in terms of opportu-nity costs if employed wives increase demands that husbands spend more time in domestic activities."

While some of the mothers I met suggested that perhaps things had changed, more mothers than fathers suggested that things haven't changed as much as they seem, or that the mes-sages were confusing, as Gloria said: "You watch television or you see movies or you read books and you think they really romanti-cize being married and how, you know, I should be walking around looking like Michelle Pfeiffer, you know, cooking in high heels and running the vacuum cleaner in my teddies . . . I think it is conflicting. They want you to be a homemaker and a lovely domestic woman, but then again they want you to look like a sex goddess and run around with red lipstick on at 7:00 in the morn-ing, and I don't think so."

In talking about differentiation in chores between husbands and wives, Morgan said, "I think a lot of that still does occur, but it's probably not as apparent as it used to be." Some wives per-ceived differentiated expectations of husbands and wives, both in terms of contributing to the domestic work and to pleasing each other:

> The wives, even if they work, are the ones that are supposed to be the housekeepers. (Whitney)

*I think they expect women to go ahead and work nine to five,
do all the chores around the house, make your husband
happy, and raise the children, like you know, the perfect
family. (Harriet)*

*I think it's still like, you know, you still have to cater to your
husband. (Margaret)*

There are links between the images of "good" mothers and
fathers and those of "good" wives and husbands. A particular kind
of "cater[ing] to," as Margaret put it, is expected of good wives,
and resembles behavior and attitudes expected of mothers. In
contrast, good husbands, like good fathers, are perceived as having a more ambiguous domestic role, although this ambiguity
is more readily acknowledged about fathers than it is about
husbands.

Nevertheless, the women I interviewed were aware of, and
therefore on some level accountable to, the notion that women
are supposed to cater to men. Men are perceived as entitled to
particular services while women are not—a notion, DeVault
(1991: 143) argues, that is based on "mostly unspoken beliefs about
relations of dominance and subordination between men and
women, and especially between husbands and wives."

DeVault points out that women often view their accommodations as choices they are making. This appeared in new mothers' discussions of changes they made in their employment that
would negatively affect their future earnings and job mobility. In
a recent follow-up interview, I was discussing this point with
Maddy and Phil, and Maddy said that she avoided looking at her
and Phil's arrangements "financially": "Maybe I'm being romantic here, but if I looked at our relationship so financially and so —
rationally might not be the right word — if I'm looking at all the
options, the relationship doesn't have as much chance of making it."

McMahon (1995: 71) argues that differences in power between
heterosexual parents are obscured by a "romantic discourse of

mutuality." Maddy went on to say that her accommodation might be naïve, that when marriages break up women are worse off financially "and the guy not necessarily, but it's the only way I know to go for it and wake up every morning and have things working out for you well in the present is to go with that positive attitude."

Some women were less adept at reframing their sacrifices, and these were the wives I spoke to who were more unhappy in the transition to parenthood. For them, parenthood may have unmasked gender imbalances in their marriage that were not acknowledged as such prior to their becoming parents. This may be a reason that gender differentiation in new parenthood is so surprising to many couples (Cowan and Cowan 1992) and why new mothers are frequently disappointed by unrealized expectations of emotional support from husbands who had not provided them with that support prior to parenthood (Belsky and Kelly 1994; Kalmuss et al. 1992). Because they do not necessarily acknowledge or recognize gender hierarchy in their marriages, couples are not prepared when it surfaces in new parenthood.

Parental Consciousness / Marital Consciousness

One of the features distinguishing many new mothers' parental consciousness is their sense of being overloaded with responsibility. Some of them spoke of their husbands as one of these responsibilities:

> *Particularly in the first year you want to give to your husband, all these people you want to give a hundred percent to, and your energy level can only go to a hundred percent. (Liza)*

> *I think the part you don't realize is that you can't do it all . . . I think that was my biggest change is knowing that I can't do everything 150 percent . . . cause I still tried to do everything at the same rate. I tried to pay as much attention to my husband, I tried to do the same amount at work, and I tried to give him [child] everything. (Laura)*

Melissa even took responsibility for creating the expectation that she would take care of Brett: "I think I'm a lot to blame for that because even when we were dating it was like I'd go out of my way to do stuff for him and it was fine when it was just the two of us but now that I have someone else who needs, requires, you know, everything from you, it's hard to give to another person on top of that."

None of the husbands in my sample expressed concerns like these in relation to their wives; that is, there was no husband who expressed discomfort about not taking care of his wife as well as he had before they had a child. This should not be a surprise, since according to Belsky and Kelly (1994), men tend to be preoccupied with themselves before they have babies, and they continue to be after they have them. To the extent that husbands talked about changes in their marriages, it was about missing time and activities with their wives. When I asked Todd about how his relationship with Peggy had changed, he said: "Very good question for a father. Very selfish answer to it. I don't feel like we had enough time together before he was born . . . There are some things that I haven't done with her that I wish I could have, probably never will."

Gil confessed that he noticed that Miranda was not taking care of him in the same way that she had before their baby Carrie was born: "It was hard to get used to at first because before it was like I was the only one, so Miranda would always do things for me . . . Even though she still tries to do it now, she's got to take care of Carrie first and she has to remind me of that every once in a while. But Carrie can't take care of herself, she has to take care of her, and that was kind of a slap in the face at first. Kind of a cold realization. But I got used to it I guess, kind of. I still have my moments." I asked him whether he can take care of himself, and he replied, "Oh yeah . . . unfortunately. Don't let Miranda know that."

As we saw, Miranda was very unhappy about her sense that Gil did not understand what her experience of new motherhood was like. Gil acknowledged that he did not often provide Miranda with much support: "I never really give Miranda much credit but she deserves a lot, trying to go to school."

"Have you said that to her, or are you just telling me?" I asked.

Gil laughed. "Actually I think usually when I try to say those kinds of things to Miranda they sort of get twisted and come out wrong and maybe lead into a little problem here or there. Maybe we get into a little argument every once in a while. But I probably don't tell her enough how much I appreciate what she does. I guess that's a common problem maybe among married people."

This commentary is consistent with Belsky's findings that new mothers miss the physical and emotional support that they had hoped to get from their husbands (but for which there was no precedent), and new fathers miss the attention that they are used to receiving from their wives: "While most new fathers expect the baby to become the main priority in the family, many are stunned at how little wifely attention or affection is left over for them. Our Project fathers complained that after the baby's arrival much less interest was shown in their work, hobbies, concerns, or sexual desires" (Belsky and Kelly 1994: 40).

I want to suggest that it is this expectation of wifely attention that plays a role in shaping gendered transitions into parenthood. If women are supposed to serve men—and there is no cultural imagery to support men serving women (DeVault 1991)—it is not a stretch to expect that women will take primary responsibility for a baby and experience stress about their husbands' loss of attention from them (see also Feldman and Nash 1984).

The rub is that not many couples acknowledge this dynamic in their own marriages. Chip, for example, preceded his observation that "the husband is usually the more dominant one and the wife is always by his side" with the qualification: "It's not in our marriage, but. . . ." Chip's description of other marriages might be apt for his own, however, given a situation that his wife Mandy anticipated. She said that leaving her paid work meant that her husband's career would now dictate the moves they made as a family; she and their child would now be in the position of relocating for Chip's career moves, and she would "gladly" do it. As DeVault (1991: 147) writes, "Indeed, for those who value some form of egalitarianism in their marriages, the requirement to serve a husband—which might be resisted if it were more explicit—is not necessarily diminished by its invisibility." The women I interviewed did not necessarily label their behavior toward their husbands as traditional wifely behavior. In many couples, however, there was a pattern of wives accommodating to husbands or feeling guilty and anxious if they didn't.

Marital Accommodation

The tendency for women to take care of men surfaced in my interviews in two areas: housework and sex. My goal in this discussion is to link the tendency for women to take primary responsibility for their babies to the tendency of many to take primary responsibility for maintaining their households and marriages. It may be that *increased* gender differentiation is an outcome of new parenthood, but the kinds of divisions of emotional and physical labor that wives and husbands have after parenthood may be embedded in their relationships to each other prior to it.

Housework is a primary realm in which men and women expect egalitarianism in marriage to take form. Yet, as many of them pointed out, it doesn't always work that way. Maddy talked about having to resist her impulse to iron her husband's shirts in the face of interactions suggesting that his appearance reflects on her: "Where Phil works it's very casual but there was one guy who always came in wrinkled and unkempt and looked like he slept in his clothes. And it's a very young company, the people are in their thirties, and they all took that as a reflection of the wife, not of him."

Brendan noted that he's "supposed to be the one" who goes grocery shopping because he likes doing it more than Eileen does, "but that doesn't seem to work out." And Todd noted that it's hard for him to hold onto the notion that he should do housework: "When she was pregnant with Jerry, I tried to do everything for her and sometimes I think I spoiled her."

"You say you think that was spoiling her?" I asked.

"Yeah at times, because it's like I feel like she just don't want to do it because she knows that I can do it and that if I can do it then she don't have to. Other times it's just I jump back into reality and say, 'Look these are things that I should be doing anyways.'"

Ted confessed that while he thought the idea of husbands and wives sharing housework was great, he felt guilty of not practicing what he preached. When I asked why he thinks it's good in theory but he doesn't in fact share housework, Ted said, "That's probably because all guys do as little as they can do. I doubt that I'm different in that way." As his comments illustrate, egalitarianism in marriage may be valued without a change in assumptions of male privilege. Equality, in this sense, is optional—something "guys" can get out of.

The role that marriage plays in gender imbalances in housework is dealt with in a growing sociological literature about divisions of household labor (see, for example, South and Spitze 1994), but my point here is to identify housework as an area in which the assumptions of heterosexual marriage may appear in a more explicit form following the birth of a baby. Ashley's comments illustrate that wives may have been picking up after husbands before they had babies, but that it somehow feels different to them after they become parents: "He's [husband] not very neat. That's our biggest argument, the one I have towards him."

"And did you used to argue about that before Dara was born?" I asked.

"No. I just picked up after him I guess, and now I have her to pick up after and I'm not picking up after him too. He should do it himself."

"Did you feel that before, that he should do it himself?"

"It never really bothered me before."

Once Ashley had a baby to take care of, taking care of her husband became too much of a burden. Although Ashley had always picked up after Bill, this accommodation was more visible to her after their baby was born.

Another area of marital relationships in which women's accommodation to men became apparent was in their postpartum interactions around sex. It is not news that new parents tend to have sex less frequently than before their babies were born, and my point in this discussion is not to focus on these changes in frequency. In fact, feeling that there was perhaps too much emphasis on sex and new parenthood, I did not originally ask the parents I interviewed about it. Yet very early on, mothers started to mention sex to me spontaneously: that they weren't having it, that they didn't want to have it, that they felt guilty about not having it. I decided that I should make a place in my interviews for both parents to address the issue, and it became something I routinely asked about.

Many of the women I interviewed spoke to feeling tired as well as experiencing a loss of desire. Margaret, who described herself as having previously enjoyed sex, said, "like, I'd rather read." Other women commented:

> We have less sex, a lot less. If you talk to him about it he'll say never. But I don't know, my body's changed since I had her [child], it's not as easy. I just don't enjoy it like I used to I guess . . . I got her, I don't want anymore [children], I guess I don't want that either. (Ashley)

> There's a lot of times I just don't have the desire. And it's not that I don't love him, it's just that Monica needs me all day. I put her to bed and I have time for myself and to get into bed, I just want to watch TV or something and then he takes it the wrong way. But I'm like, "You don't understand. If you stayed with her for a few days." (Melissa)

While women tended to take responsibility for not having sex, and to wonder, as Sylvia did, "if it's going to take its toll" on their marriages, Sylvia's husband Sean told me that he didn't necessarily let Sylvia know that he was tired too: "I think that it's both of us. I think maybe sometimes it's Sylvia a little more, and maybe she believes it's her. Maybe there's some times with my male ego that I let her think that rather than admit that I'm really tired." When I asked if he had told her that, he said, "No."

Several women spoke to feeling guilty about turning down their husbands' sexual overtures, and some had sex when they did not really want to. Whitney described a period of time during which she did not enjoy having sex with her husband because their baby would be crying in the next room during their love-making: "It didn't bother him. He could let her cry . . . After she was born, we had to get TV upstairs because upon her crying, he would immediately switch the TV on. If we were going to make love or whatever, it would kind of drown out the sound . . . I would make love anyway even though I wasn't really there and then I felt worse after. It's like I would jump right out of bed and go in there and he knew I was going to do that."

Whitney accommodated Bob despite her own discomfort, and other women made similar gestures to their husbands. Liza talked about how she came to realize that her disinterest in sex had been a form of neglect of her husband Peter: "And I try to tell him that, I say, 'Peter, I don't think I'm the only one having these problems.'" I asked if she experienced this as more her problem than his and she said, "Yeah. . . . Peter has a lot of physical stamina, more than I have. I think I didn't perceive it as a problem. I pushed it under the carpet, you know, my neglect for my husband."

Maddy described her sense of obligation to "buck up" and push through her fatigue and physical pain to have sex with her husband:

> I think there are times in a relationship where even though you are tired, you buck up. And sometimes you do and sometimes you don't, and when you don't, you feel kind of cruddy about it. Sometimes you don't and that's fine. Sometimes you say, "I'm tired, sorry," and that's okay too. But there are times when you really feel you should be putting a little more energy into it and you just don't . . . I didn't turn him down,

but what happened, and I don't know why this is, because it just seems incredible to me that you can give birth and then have sex be painful, but it was for a while. So we would both be sort of nervous about it. Should we try again, or is it going to be bad again? It was sort of not satisfactory for either side and yet we both sort of, or at least I had the impression that that was the only thing that would ultimately make it better and not hurt, was that you try and you ease into it.

The fathers I spoke to did not tend to complain explicitly about changes in their sexual interactions with their wives, as Bill illustrates: "I try to understand the way she feels because she just doesn't have the urge since she had the baby so, I mean what are we going to do, you know? So as far as that goes, I try to respect, I mean I do go nuts every once in a while, but I'd say overall I like the relationship better the way it is now."

Other fathers said similar things — that they felt closer to their wives than they had before, even though their relationships had become less sexual. When it came to talking about sex, the men I interviewed were less open with me than the women were — often not taking me up on the opportunity I presented to talk about changes in their sexual relationships with their partners or addressing it very briefly. Either their female partners had less to feel guilty about than they thought, or only a few fathers felt comfortable in talking with me about sex. I suspect it was a little of both.[2]

The dynamic I have presented — of some wives feeling obliged to accommodate their husbands sexually — is valid I believe, but I do not know how conscious husbands were of it. For example, the husband whose wife reported that he turned up the TV while their baby cried did not tell me about that from his point of view. To the extent that some fathers did express frustration with the state of their sexual relationships with their wives, only one discussed it in any detail. More often, it was indirect — like Bill, slipping in a side comment ("I do go nuts every once in a while"), or Jay, who told me that he and his best friend complain to each other about not being able to get a date (a military euphemism for "have sex"). But he mentioned this in the context of describing his friendship — not when I asked specifically about his relationship with his wife.

My point is to suggest that wives' postpartum responses to both housework and sex illustrate dynamics of accommodation and caretaking of husbands. The notion that women should be selfless caregivers who serve their families shapes their negotiation of parenthood with their husbands (as well as leading them to pick up after them and provide them with sex). What is less clear from my data is how much husbands explicitly demanded this of their wives or whether it was simply structured into their marriages, in the way that the implications of men's better paychecks often were.

I emphasize wives' responsiveness to husbands because, as I mentioned before, other researchers have stressed women's roles in keeping men out of parenting. Belsky and Kelly (1994: 36, 244), for example, write that a woman may be "so critical of her husband's parenting that, without intending to, she drives him away." They also suggest that mothers are responsible for keeping their husbands connected to their children. Women will strive to be good parents "no matter what" while men's good parenting is contingent on their feelings about their wives. Marital unhappiness will therefore create distance between a man and his child, Belsky and Kelly suggest, because his commitment to his child is generated by his connection to his wife rather than by any direct sense of connection to his baby.

Other people make this argument as well, but it is one that I am resistant to because I think it sells men short on their capacities to attach to their children. It also provides a kind of rationale for fathers not to support their children should their marriages end. I think if we conceptualize involved fatherhood as important (and possible), fathers will construct their relationships to their children differently and take responsibility for them — with or without female partners. For example, more than 90 percent of fathers with joint custody of their children pay child support as opposed to the 43 percent of fathers who have no visitation rights (Rubiner 1997). On a different note, more intense fathering could lead fathers to greater commitment to their families, and perhaps a decrease in divorce (Schwartz 1994).

Cowan and Cowan (1992) identify a "marital dance" in which paternal involvement is discouraged, and imply that it is the women who are leading this dance. They suggest that full-time mothers may feel threatened by their husbands' involvement and push them out of contact with their babies.[3] They note that mothers intervene in interactions between their husbands and babies in ways that reinforce the notion that they have greater expertise than their husbands. And they suggest that full-time mothers' concerns with not losing their special role leads them to ambivalence about their husbands' contributions to baby care. Whether mothers are playing the expert or responding to their own sense of inadequacy, they are perceived as responsible for fathers' retreat from baby care.

Even people who believe that economic inequality is reinforced by women having primary responsibility for children suggest that mothers have the power and responsibility to reshape parenting roles. Mahony (1995: 238) calls on women to "redefine motherhood in their own hearts" and share the care of babies with fathers in the interest of achieving economic equality. She suggests that if women act in ways to improve their bargaining positions with their male partners, they will be able to influence the division of child care. In other words, it is up to mothers to implement a program to engage fathers in the care of their children.[4] Yet, as the old saying goes, you can lead a horse to water, but you can't make him drink. What I'm suggesting here is that the horses are often more in charge than the people who have been conceptualized as holding the reins.

New Parenthood and Marital Power Imbalances

One of the arguments I am making in this chapter is that gender differentiation, and particularly the accommodation of husbands by wives, appears to precede as well as to follow new parenthood. There are particular variables, however, such as emotional or economic dependence, that may mediate the balance of power in marriages. Women's possible advantages in these power areas may be at an all-time low after they become mothers (see also Mahony 1995), although many do not think of these changes as losses. In fact, because of their accountability to images of good mothering, they may willingly change their economic status, which is the example with which I begin.

In most societies, women's power increases as their ability to be self-supporting increases (Epstein 1988). Economic power has been identified as a key variable in women's positions relative to their husbands (Blumberg and Coleman 1989). Employment and earnings have also been identified as factors in divisions of family work (Coltrane 1996; Sanchez and Thomson 1997). In the group of new parents I interviewed, about half of the mothers had gone from having full-time employment to working part-time or not working at all.

Even when women did not leave their paid jobs completely, their parental consciousness influenced how they approached these jobs. These kinds of changes in power dynamics may be masked for women who perceive the realignment as simply part of doing what is best for their child (see Komter 1989 on latent and invisible power in "egalitarian" marriages; see also LaRossa and LaRossa 1989). Laura let go of one part of her job that she had enjoyed because she did not want to see Nicky at the babysitter for longer hours. She did not, however, question the hours necessary for Stuart's job.

Economic power alone does not necessarily undo gender hierarchy. Harriet, for example, made more money than her husband, but said that she thought it was important for the man to be "the head of the household" (see also Hochschild 1989). LaRossa and LaRossa (1989) suggest that wives' power decreases in the transition to parenthood *regardless* of employment status, because of the unrelenting demands of babies. Wives may become more dependent on husbands because they need them in order to be able to take breaks from their physical (if not their mental) responsibility for their babies. Often their parental consciousness will dictate that their husbands are the best—though not equal—substitutes for them. Laura said, "When my husband was home I didn't have a care in the world because I knew at least he [child] was with Daddy."

So, while wives may resent their husbands' greater freedom, as Laura said she did, they nevertheless must appreciate and reinforce their husbands for the amount that they are willing to do. LaRossa and LaRossa (1989: 146) write that even though a wife may not like that her husband's relief of her is defined as a gift, she won't "cut off the aid"; husbands may even increase their wives' sense of dependency by pointing out how much more baby care they do than their male friends.

When couples experience conflict about housework, it is generally not simply about who does what, but about who should be grateful to whom (Hochschild 1989: 18). This "economy of gratitude," Hochschild suggests, relates to how individuals define what should be expected of them as men and women. Applying this notion to baby care: If taking responsibility for a baby is defined as "women's work," there is no reason for a man to feel grateful if his wife does it. If fathers are seen as doing mothers a favor when they participate in baby care, fathers will receive more appreciation from their partners than they give back, which may contribute to wives feeling more emotionally dependent on their husbands, though not necessarily emotionally supported.

For some women the economy of gratitude includes having had a baby at all. Harriet described how her friends remind her to let her husband know that he is important: "Once in a while I have a good conversation with one of my girlfriends who's got kids and she says, 'Remember your husband came first. He did. Without him you don't have children. Without him you don't really have a family.'"

Belsky and Kelly (1994) suggest that what couples need in order to weather the transition to parenthood successfully is "mutual empathy"; that is, men need to recognize their wives' needs for support and women need to recognize their husbands' needs for attention.[5] Advice givers are not necessarily immune, however, to images of marriage as an institution that is stabilized by wives' accommodations to their husbands. Hays (1996) notes that Dr. Spock advises mothers to remember to pay some attention to their husbands, while not making an equivalent comment to fathers. In *What to Expect the First Year* (Eisenberg et al. 1989: 582–583), the following advice is given: "The period of new parenthood is actually one during which it is very easy for couples to grow apart instead of closer. Yet your relationship with your husband is the most significant in your life — more important even than the relationship with your child . . . So give your relationship its due now and make a conscious effort to keep the love-lights glowing or, if they seem to have flickered out, to rekindle them."

These authors make clear that women are the ones who should make the effort to keep relationships with men "glowing." Notice, however, that they do not suggest doing the tango — because everyone knows that takes two.

Aside from these kinds of socialization messages, dynamics in which wives accommodate to husbands are reinforced by pay inequity, occupational segregation, and other forms of gender stratification. These structural arrangements assume and reinforce divisions of labor in which women take primary responsibility for families (Reskin and Padavic 1994), and mitigate against wives keeping an equal foothold in their marriages (if they previously had one). As Sylvia said of her marriage, "I think we are pretty much liberated but I still find that we are falling into a lot of the common sort of roles . . . It's just hard to necessarily escape it because I don't think the support systems are built there yet in society."

Among the support systems that are missing are fair pay for women and an appreciation of "women's work." Not only would this create more debate between mothers and fathers about who should leave their job or cut back their hours, but a greater valuing of caregiving, in both its paid and unpaid forms, might change the choices that parents have and make in juggling their employment and families—and thus change the balance of caregiving between husbands and wives.

I have suggested in this chapter that gendered parental consciousness is an underrated influence on the tensions that arise between married couples following the birth of a baby. These differences in consciousness are reproduced, in part, through residue of gender difference and hierarchy embedded in heterosexual marriage as an institution. But like parenthood, and gender in general, marriage is something that women and men accomplish together. So it is possible, with conscious effort and even in the context of structural obstacles, to attain equity if that is what a couple values. And there is research indicating that when men and women share parenting, their marital relationships are enhanced (Coltrane 1996; Ehrensaft 1990; Schwartz 1994).

CHAPTER 6

❦

Images of Family

IT SEEMS ALMOST TOO OBVIOUS TO SAY, BUT NEW PAR-
ents' approaches to parenting are influenced by both their
past and present family experiences and interactions. How
this influence operates, however, is not so obvious. Unlike dilemmas such as how to feed babies or what to do about employment,
new parents do not necessarily decide whether to respond to their
families at any given moment, yet family upbringings — or what
Cowan and Cowan (1992) refer to as family "legacies" — serve as
a powerful and complicated reference point for new parents' approaches to motherhood and fatherhood.

Many theories about gender differences, and about differences in parenting in particular, root their analysis in the notion
that early childhood experiences are a determining factor in how
women and men approach parenthood. This argument is made
in different forms by sociologists as well as by psychologists, each
of whom discuss the role of past family experiences in shaping
future families. Belsky and Kelly (1994: 31) suggest, for example,
that differences in upbringing "give men and women contrasting
ideas of what it means to be a parent." Cowan and Cowan (1992)

note that it is difficult for men to shake the notion that child rearing is "women's work" because most of them were raised primarily by their mothers.

The fact that mothers tend to be the primary parents of children is the underpinning for Nancy Chodorow's (1978) psychoanalytic analysis of how parenting styles are created through children's identification with their own parents. Her discussion of how mothers reproduce themselves in their daughters is an attempt at explaining the perpetuation of a gendered division of labor in child care. Chodorow's argument is that women's exclusive investment in mothering reproduces in daughters a new generation of women who will also experience motherhood as a sole and insufficient source of self-esteem and personal accomplishment. Because mothers are denied outlets in the public sphere and isolated from relationships with other adults, they become overly invested in their children. Girls identify with their mothers, and boys must *not* identify with their mothers, in order to achieve their appropriate gender roles; boys therefore devalue the caretaking behavior that they associate with femaleness.

Making use of Chodorow's theory, Richards (1982: 70) suggests that because fathers are connected with the world outside of home, they represent from birth "separateness and detachment." Men's socialization, Richards argues, reproduces distance in fathers across generations. It "prepares them for a world of male superiority in which they will strive in the world of work and remain withdrawn from the emotional world of family and children."[1]

There are other possible explanations for the male dominance and female devaluation that Chodorow roots in mothering. Miriam Johnson (1988) has pointed to the socialization of girls toward being wives as well as male peer group culture as influences. And social learning theorists argue that many socialization experiences, beyond the mother/daughter dyad, reinforce girls when they imitate mothering behavior (Boyd 1989).

Despite these responses to Chodorow's particular account, research about mother/daughter relationships suggests that for women who are becoming mothers, their own mothers, in some way, may facilitate the transition (Fischer 1988). Minimally, mothers serve as reference points for their daughters' ideas about motherhood. But this occurs in more diverse ways than are suggested by the theory that daughters simply identify with and reproduce their mothers in themselves.[2] Further, there is evidence suggesting that prospective mothers' intentions do not adequately explain their later experiences. Lucy Rose Fischer (1991) finds, for example, that despite the fact that adult daughters in her research often viewed their mothers in negative terms, those with children were more than twice as likely as those without children to see their lives as replicating their mothers'. About the attitudes of adult daughters in her study, she notes: "Either they saw resemblances to their mothers as a tainted inheritance (characteristics that they did *not* want) and/or they insisted that their lives were or would be very different from their mothers' lives" (Fischer 1991: 241).

Families have also been identified as a specific source of messages for new parents during the actual transition to parenthood. For example, Cowan and Cowan (1992: 104) suggest that grandparents may experience less gender-differentiated approaches to parenting as "a threat or implied criticism of the 'old way' of family making." They describe intergenerational tension between men and their parents when new fathers try to take a more active role with their children than their fathers did. Coltrane (1996: 146) also suggests that for couples attempting to share parenting, contact with kin may create pressure "to conform to the elders' more conventional standards."

Present-Day Family Interactions

It was apparent in Chapter 4 that family relationships were one of the sites through which various messages were conveyed to new parents about the meanings associated with their biological experiences. Many of the parents I interviewed mentioned sisters, mothers, and in-laws in discussing their approaches to the breast-versus-bottle debate. Liza was discouraged from breast-feeding by her sister's experience, for example. Melissa, on the other hand, felt that she had to match her sister's breast-feeding or she would be a worse mother. Brett's mother warned him that Melissa's hormones might make her crazy, which was how Brett interpreted Melissa's marital dissatisfaction.

Eileen's comments in Chapter 2 also illustrated the influence of interactions with her parents during her transition into parenthood, and in particular, their ability to generate guilt in her about how she was doing as a mother. Her father made a comment that implied that she was smothering Jimmy, and her mother commented that she should be glad that Jimmy knows who she is — the implication being that Eileen's employment put this knowledge at risk.

What is interesting for this discussion is that prior to telling me the story about visiting her parents, Eileen had commented that it was important to her that Jimmy understand who she is. In other words, Eileen was accountable to the idea that her special role in Jimmy's life might be jeopardized by her not being with him all the time — an idea that had either been generated or echoed by her mother. New parents' interactions with mothers and mothers-in-law in particular may reinforce anxiety and a sense of responsibility in new mothers as well as sustain the image of parenting as "women's work."

Some mothers described feeling evaluated by their mothers. For Alison, this was positive. Her mother had baby-sat and told Alison how well-behaved her child was. "She was genuinely impressed," Alison said, "That made me feel really good." In other cases, however, mothers did not support or even actively criticized their daughters. Melissa commented: "My mother always used to say, 'I hope you have one just like yourself,' because I was very difficult when I was a baby. And Monica was the same way . . . I know it's horrible to say, but yeah, I think she thinks I got a taste of my own medicine." Ashley said of her mother: "Like I'll go over there and she'll grab her [child] right out of my arms and like, 'Oh you should have a tee shirt on her, oh you should have shoes on her, you should have these kind of shoes on her, you should do this for her, you're feeding her all wrong, she's not eating right.' Just everything."

Ashley was ambivalent about what she saw as her mother's taking control: "She's a pain, but she's always there for me though." Ashley's husband, Bill, shared this ambivalence: "Her mother means well, she's really nice and really helpful, but she does annoy me sometimes." Bill described how his mother-in-law's possessiveness of her granddaughter, Dara, led her to make "little digs" at him. He described coming home early from work one day and going over to the baby-sitter's house to see Dara. Ashley and her mother pulled up in a car, and as Dara was walking over to Bill, his mother-in-law said, "She don't want to walk to you." Bill interpreted this as jealousy of his relationship with his daughter. Whatever it was, it did not reflect an affirmation of this father's close relationship with his daughter.

The scrutiny and sense of ownership of children that some new mothers in my research perceived from family members did not necessarily enhance their parenting. Maggie described herself as always losing patience with her son, Kevin, when she was at the home of Joel's mother: "I was going to sit everyone down and say, 'Look. I am Kevin's mother. Whether you think I'm a good mother or not, I am.' I felt like his whole family didn't think that I was a good mother."

Joel's mother spent a lot of time baby-sitting for Kevin, and there were struggles between her and Maggie about what Kevin should eat and wear: "I would come home crying because, 'I just can't believe you don't put a hat on that child! I mean, don't you worry about him?' Blah blah, just constant."

Maggie said that she thought it was hard for Joel "because most of the digs at me, whenever something was said, he was never around. He was always at work." Joel therefore did not intervene with his mother and grandmother on Maggie's behalf: "He felt like everything was hearsay . . . Like that he had to be there. And really I guess I don't blame him, but now he's started to stick up for me."

Miranda also described disagreements with her husband's

mother: "She tells me that I should beat my child and that I should do this and that." When I talked to Gil about tensions between his wife and mother, he said, "I think it was just on differing opinions." I asked where he came into that; he responded that he tries not to, and laughed. He did, later, express sadness about the situation: "It doesn't help that we're so far away but then feeling that you kind of have this little wedge between you because you love both of them. You really can't choose sides about it. I married Miranda. I've got to spend the rest of my life with her. Kind of hard."

It was notable that Gil experienced his dilemma as one in which he had to choose between his loyalties to his mother and to his daughter's mother. This approach reflected an adherence to the notion of parenting as "women's work," and Gil was trying not to have to decide which woman was right. He perceived the disagreement between his mother and his wife about how to approach his daughter's behavior as something that he could not "choose sides" about, despite the fact that the debate was partly about whether Carrie should be beaten. To not assert an opinion about corporal punishment seemed an especially stark example of avoiding parental responsibility; but from Gil's perspective, it was a loyalty issue. In another part of my interview with him, Gil indicated that he and Miranda had agreed not to hit their daughter (Miranda had won this one); nevertheless he kept his own voice out of the debate between the two women.

The kinds of dynamics that I have described only emerged for me as I was analyzing family data well after I had completed my interviews. This is therefore an incomplete discussion of the impact of current interactions with parents and in-laws, because it was an area that I did not probe during the data collection process. When I went back over my interviews, however, I was struck by how dynamics such as these could fuel new mothers' insecurity and sense of responsibility as well as new fathers' sense of being more peripheral as a parent.

I also think that the sparseness of my data may reflect the relative invisibility of the role that families play in reinforcing a gendered status quo. A brief comment from Laura suggested this to me as I was rereading interview transcripts. Laura had just been talking about her impression that new mothers experience more change in their lives than new fathers do. After noting that she doesn't know why that happens, Laura said, "I was talking to my mom about it and she just, she's like, 'Oh, that's just the way it is.'"

Perhaps that is the lesson that many new parents get in their families: That's just the way it is. The way that new parents interpret how their past family experiences influenced their images of good mothering and fathering also suggests that that's just the way it *was*. In fact, Maddy commented in a recent follow-up interview that she wonders if her relationship with Phil is more equal because they both were raised by single parents, and "neither one of us saw a relationship as we were growing up."

INTERPRETATIONS OF PAST FAMILY EXPERIENCES

One of the questions I routinely asked the parents I interviewed was whether they thought of anyone in particular when they thought of their own image of a good mother or father. About one-half of the parents mentioned their own mothers in talking about good mothers, while less than one-third mentioned their fathers in connection to their images of a good father.

Fathers who were remembered as good fathers were those who worked hard and spent time with their families when they could. Ruth said of her dad, for example: "He was a very good father, provided for us. He worked a great deal . . . He took us whenever he had to go someplace on business and we were on vacation and he took us with him."

Mothers were remembered as good in ways that conformed to the image of the ever-present, ever-patient mother, as Sarah recalls: "I never remember being spanked or yelled at. My mother used to sit me down and talk, and I can remember thinking, 'I just wish she'd spank me.'"

The memory of a mother who was "always there" was mentioned by a number of people—some because their mothers were literally home most of the time—but others thought of their employed mothers as "the type of person who was always there," which is how Laura described her mother: "She spent a lot of time with us as kids. I mean I think she did work, but I don't remember her working as much as about her being at home."

Miranda described the economic trade-off that her mother made in leaving her job to take care of her children: "She lost a lot of money in retirement that she could have had, but she was there, and she's still there." This equation of economic sacrifice with being a mother who is "there" is a theme that turns up in approaches to maternal employment in Chapter 7.

When fathers were criticized, it was for being absent. When mothers were criticized, it was for being *too* present. Barbara said of her mother: "My mom was almost too involved and now still wants to be too involved. She has to think about her life and get on with her life and I would hope that I'd keep my own life."

Harriet, whose mother had become seriously ill, said, "As much as I've always pictured her to be a strong person, I realize now that she wasn't quite as strong as I thought. It isn't a disappointment to me, but I just feel that now she's kind of let down the family in a way by not taking care of herself." While criticizing her mother's selflessness, Harriet wanted more from her father: "I just wish that my father was more involved, took an interest in things that I did. I mean I played volleyball, I played softball, and he never once came to a game."

Good mothers were perceived as setting a standard their daughters might not be able to reach, while sons generally compared favorably with their fathers:

> *My dad drove a truck a lot so he was out on the road a lot. I remember missing him. I try to be more involved with Dylan in that aspect. (Jay)*

> *I think I'm more involved than my father probably was. My father . . . would not change more than four or five diapers a week. (Brendan)*

After saying that his father only changed a few diapers a week, Brendan added, "I'm not sure if I change many more than that."

But if he did change more diapers than his father had, he had characterized himself as more involved than his father was, which was what Eileen had pointed out about the model being different for fathers than for mothers.

Some mothers recognized that they could not meet the standards their mothers had set. Barbara said, "I don't think I could compare myself to the levels that my mom did. She wasn't working outside the home. Her job really was raising the kids." But other mothers strongly identified with the image of having primary responsibility for taking care of their children, husband, and home—as their mothers had—and they felt their idealization of what their mothers had done for them as a source of pressure. Andrea said, "I think of my mother and just how much guidance and everything she's offered me, so that sometimes sends me into a panic. And then I'm really proud of my mother and I really adore her and I would do anything for her. Then sometimes I worry, and I'm like, 'Oh gosh, do you think Jessica will feel this way about me?'" Miranda spoke to feeling that she had to "fill my mom's shoes": "She was not as happy when the house was a mess. She'd be like, 'I have to do this and this and this, you know, the house is dirty, oh boy, and your dad's going to be home.'"

This kind of dynamic was being replicated in the households of Miranda and Gil, and Andrea and Wade. Andrea described her employment decisions as hinging, in part, on her and Wade's belief that it is important for a family to have dinner together. Miranda experienced the same kind of stress anticipating her husband's arrival home as her mother had. Her expectations for herself were generated in part by the "very, very happy" childhood Miranda perceived herself as having had, in which gendered images of her parents were embedded: "My dad built a playhouse in our backyard. My mom would bring little peanut-butter-and-jelly sandwiches to me and my friends when we were playing. She was hanging her clothes on the clothesline, doing her thing." Like Miranda, Andrea modeled her expectations for her division of labor with her husband on what her mother had done: "My mother was really the one who I felt raised us. So with Wade's schedule . . . that's what I'm accustomed to." Miranda and

Andrea evaluated their lives based on the precedents their mothers had set.

The precedent set by their fathers that several men mentioned—aside from providing economically—was being available for sports. Sports may be the one area in which boys experience more direct contact with fathers who are generally absent or distant emotionally (Messner 1992). New fathers talked about their availability to their children in terms of whether their work schedules would permit their attendance at their children's (future) sporting events.

Men's images of good fathering frequently contained allusions to sports. David said of the grandfather he thought of as his father: "He has always looked out for me and for us. I mean he's the one who taught me to play baseball and football." Jay said that the only time his father was involved with him was around sports: "Dad was involved with me when it came to the athletics, and then after the athletics, it was pretty much Mom." For Jay, his connection with his father concerning athletics was ambivalent: "My dad was a big college football player, and he didn't force me into it, but like right now my dad can still quote you high school and college football scores and stuff like that. And I can't do that; I'm gonna try not to force Dylan."

Just as some women negotiated certain images from their mothers, some men confronted messages about their adequacy from their fathers:

> *He always wanted me to be doing something that I wasn't doing. Other than that, I was always making the wrong choices. (Tom)*

> *My father was a little tougher than I would have liked him to be, especially when I was younger. . . . I don't think that that's bad. He just expected a lot. I'll probably do the same types of things. (Jake)*

Jake's prediction that he would replicate his father's toughness was something with which Todd was struggling. On one hand, Todd said that by physically abusing him, his father had "made me a man." On the other hand, he recognized that it had given him "things to worry about": "It's like second nature to me that I have to think constantly, you know, 'Calm down. Gather yourself.'"

Todd expressed disappointment that his mother, who had done so much for him, had not been strong enough to stand up to his father: "My mother did everything for me but never did the things that she should have . . . She tried to do the best for me and show me the right way, even though she was under the thumb I guess you could say. She never said anything when my father had words with me or raised his hand to me. She was sort of like scared."

In contrast to his mother, Todd explained that his wife, Peggy, does intervene with him on their son's behalf: "I don't really spank him. I give him a tap here and there, but she sees it and it's like appalling, you know, so if she feels like it's appalling, I'll always respect her wishes." He went on to say that he loves that Peggy "stands for what she believes in. I guess unlike her, that's one thing I hated about my mother."

While watching a child be physically abused should hardly be condoned, it was notable that Todd in some way held his mother responsible for his father's actions. And while it was clear that he knew that he had to take responsibility for cooling off in interactions with his own son, he gave Peggy credit for identifying his behavior as unacceptable. In both generations, Todd imbued mothers with the responsibility to oversee fathers. In the same way that Todd expected Peggy to tell him to change a diaper, he also looked to her to control his physical punishment of their child. Todd told me that he learned that what he had experienced from his father was abuse when he heard similar behavior described as abuse on a talk show.

MEDIA MESSAGES AND THE INSTITUTIONAL REPRODUCTION OF "THE FAMILY"

I suggest in this section that there are two ways that past and current television media provide institutional reinforcement for gendered images of parents.[3] The first is that the television programs that the parents I interviewed grew up watching provided particular images of what mothers and fathers are supposed to be. The second is that television programming that they currently watch reinforces a sense of negative consequences when people stray from these gendered expectations.

The television shows that many new parents watched while they were growing up provided images of "good" families with gendered approaches to parenthood. Whether it was the extended family of *The Waltons* or the nuclear family of *Leave It to Beaver* or *The Brady Bunch* stepfamily, the mothers were nurturing, patient moms and the fathers were productive, though relatively domestically inept, dads. Phil referred to this as "the Donna Reed view of parenting": "The mother, that's what she does . . . and the father being kind of semidetached, floating above the fray."

Fictional television mothers and fathers were part of the consciousness of many of the people I interviewed. It was not uncommon for someone to ask me if I knew a particular television character or family in an effort to describe something about themselves or their family. In fact, several people, in response to the question of who they think of as a "good" mother or father, mentioned parents from television: Mr. Brady, Papa Walton, Timmy's mom from *Lassie*, June Cleaver. The parents in these families provided a source of comparison for their own parents, as in Maggie's case: "My mom was working and I would think she wasn't home that much in the morning. I think she left, she got me up for school, and then she had to go to work. So it wasn't like we had a family breakfast or anything like that. You know, cramming a Pop-tart — it wasn't, you know, like that June Cleaver."

Some people, like Maddy, who had grown up without fathers, described how television supplied them with ideas of what fathers were supposed to be like: "I didn't have one and I sort of assumed that they were all Ward Cleavers and whoever was on TV at the time."

While current television programming was not perceived as generating many positive images of parenting, Eileen suggested that it conveys the consequences of not conforming to the good mother model: "I think that television and movies and media portray the consequences of not being the model more than they portray the model . . . This is what happens when you aren't that." Liza illustrated this concept. In describing her concern about whether she would be supportive enough to her child—if he has a bad day, "will I say the right thing?" —Liza talked about her fear of being like the parents on television talk shows: "You know, you watch the Oprahs and you watch the Montels and stuff, and you see these horrible parents, and it's like, how can they do that to children, you know?"

The one current television family show that several fathers liked was *Home Improvement*, starring comedian Tim Allen. Brett commented that *Home Improvement* was one of the few programs that "show parents as role models." According to Jay, the show portrayed an "average family" that "is still a little traditionalist": "She is more of the homemaker even though I think she has a job . . . You know what Tim Allen's job is and she is always the one cooking dinner and she is always the one telling Tim how to do the children." Bill commented, "It gives you the comedic side of how men and women don't always get along, you know, things do bother them, but you don't see the family coming apart."

At the time of the writing of this book, *Home Improvement* is one of the most popular shows on television. An article about its star, Tim Allen, cites his "retro view of the sexes" as the reason he is the season's "hottest funnyman." At the conclusion of an interview with Allen, he comments about what he refers to as "gender wars": "This stuff's not going to change. Women are going to have babies and they're going to have feelings that men aren't going to feel. Just because a man stays home as a househusband, that doesn't mean he has the same feelings a woman has for kids" (*USA Weekend*, 1994: 6).

It may be that part of the appeal of the show is that rather than giving the couples in my study the current idealized image of egalitarian parenting arrangements, it reflects what is really happening in their households. Having moved from the happy gender differentiation of Ward and June Cleaver, now there are Tim and Jill Taylor, whose gender differentiation generates arguments, but who nevertheless stay together. Perhaps the only idealized part is how funny it always seems to be.

The way that families are portrayed on television reinforces a view that children and marriages are best served when men focus on bringing home the bacon and women are in charge of frying it up in the pan (to use an image favored by several of the people I interviewed). At the same time that television shows reinforce this split between domestic and "productive" work, they also imply that the split does not influence the physical presence of family members; that is, everybody tends to be home.

Some people struggled with this contradiction. In talking about her loneliness with trying to be a good mother and her anticipation of Gil (who was in the military) having to leave for several months, Miranda cried and said, "Normally this is not something I cry about. Normally I love to talk about family and husband and child and all that." Miranda's upset was induced perhaps by her idea that "family and husband and child and all that" all go together when that wasn't really her day-to-day, and soon, her month-to-month experience. "Family" to her was supposed to mean a physical partnership between a man and a woman that was unlike what she was experiencing.

Blending an image of family with gender differentiation was also problematic for Melissa. Although she and Brett were consciously recreating the image of family that they had gotten in their families of origin, Melissa was more stressed by her end of the bargain than Brett was by his. On one hand, Melissa believed that mothers belong at home with their children: "My mom stayed home and one thing that always meant a great deal, when we got off the bus, we always knew that we were going home to somebody." But at the same time, her image of family included Brett's presence, and she found herself anticipating the weekends when Brett would be home: "You don't want to feel like you're the only person bringing these kids up, plus you want to have it like a unit where you're together with your husband, the family is together, even if it's just for a day."

"Family" as an Accomplishment

While some theorists attribute gendered parenting arrangements to early childhood experiences, others argue that gender is created in interactions and opportunities throughout the life span.[4] Families are a source of interactions that may reinforce gendered transitions into parenthood, in part, simply by not posing a challenge to them. Brett said, "I don't think of it too much. Fortunately Melissa's parents are together, my parents are together, so we don't know any different than this is what you do. You get married, you find a job." I commented, "You're doing what you do." Brett replied, "What my parents did. Yeah basically, trying to . . . That's the only thing I know, so I'm comfortable that way, and Melissa is comfortable that way." As we've already seen, Melissa was less comfortable than Brett was, but they did share a commitment to upholding this family arrangement.

People who had families that did not fit the norm were nevertheless aware of what mothers, fathers, and families were supposed to look like. Many of them experienced their differences as deviations rather than simply as differences. These interpretations were reinforced on an institutional level by the way that families are portrayed in visual media. Many television shows reproduce dominant images of "good" mothering and fathering while not accurately reflecting the implications of the gender differentiation they celebrate. Television moms and dads have different responsibilities, yet they always seem to be together. The parents I interviewed who did the differentiation couldn't necessarily pull off the togetherness.

❦

CHAPTER 7

Employment, Child Care, and Parental Accountability

A S MUCH OF THIS BOOK REFLECTS, ONE OF THE primary ways in which new mothers and fathers define themselves and confront social definitions of motherhood and fatherhood is through their relationships to paid work. While employment is seen as an obvious element of good fathering, it poses more of a challenge to the expectations of availability and exclusivity that underlie imagery associated with good mothers. Employment necessitates absence of mothers from their babies, and that absence necessitates caregiving from people other than mothers.

The experiences of motherhood and employment are affected by the notions that the ideal for both is full-time and exclusive attention. "Working mothers" are therefore suspected of neglecting their children, and employees who are mothers are suspected of neglecting their work (Lewis 1991). Some researchers have found that increased participation of mothers with young children in the labor force in the 1970s brought a greater acceptance of women combining family and paid work (Nock 1987). But others suggest that the equation of men with work and women with home is "surprisingly impervious" to labor market changes (Coltrane 1996: 26). In any case, the incorporation of the notion that mothers can be employed has happened without the recognition that the demands of both mothering and working might need modification (Lewis 1991).[1]

Against this ideological backdrop is the lingering question in empirical literature—why is it that new mothers are, or are not, employed? This question is not asked of new fathers, nor have the effects of new fathers' work statuses on their babies been explored anywhere as profusely as the effects of new mothers' work statuses (see McKee 1982; see also Scarr et al. 1989 and Spitze 1988 for surveys of research about maternal employment). What we do know about work and the transition to fatherhood is that parenthood does not affect men's employment activities as much as it does women's (Sanchez and Thomson 1997).[2] If anything, some research suggests that parenthood tends to increase men's employment activities (Waite et al. 1985), and that fathers' status as wage earners may give them more discretion in whether and how they provide direct care to their babies.[3] In other words, fathers are not asked why they are employed; rather, they are asked why they "help" with the hands-on care of their babies.[4]

On the other hand, fathers are generally denied a choice between fatherhood and employment (Gerson 1991). Cowan and Cowan (1992) point to the economics and organization of workplaces, as well as the lack of quality nonparental child care, as encouraging fathers to work and mothers to stay home. They also note the financial burden created by differences between men's and women's wages when both parents try to maintain employment and be home more. These practical realities shape fathers' definitions of their responsibilities, directing them more toward financial provision.

But that is only part of the story, as Marsiglio (1993) points out, since individual fathers can and do challenge typical patterns. In some cases, finances provide a justification for reverting to a more gendered division of labor, as in Ehrensaft's sample of sharing parents in which the most often cited reason for a shift in fifty-fifty time commitment to parenting was financial. She notes that this may be either a rationalization or a legitimate explanation; in her view, it was a combination of both.

As it turns out, the influence most cited by new mothers to explain their employment behavior is that which is assumed for fathers: financial need. While other factors such as personal enjoyment and career development are also mentioned by new mothers, financial need is the most important reason given for returning to work within three months after an infant's birth (Volling and Belsky 1993). Although it may be more socially acceptable for mothers to say that they leave their babies out of economic need, women married to full-time breadwinners have the largest reductions in employment after motherhood (Sanchez and Thomson 1997), and it does appear that mothers who contribute more to the total family income tend to return to work more quickly (Wenk and Garrett 1992). Mothers are also more apt to return to work when they receive maternity benefits: "The assurance of job security after childbirth, coupled with financial need, prompts most women with maternity benefits to return to work rapidly" (Coltrane 1996: 212).

Other variables that have been examined in the quest to understand the employment behavior of new mothers include personality characteristics, sex role attitudes, and the level of a woman's expressed interest in a job or career (see Morgan and Hock 1984; Behrman 1982; McHale and Huston 1984). One study found that women who expect to stay home believe that their babies are distressed by their absence while women who expect to be employed believe that this causes no direct stress to their babies. Other women, less consistent in their attitudes, assess their opportunities once their babies are born, and having arrived at a home or work path, "array their perceptions of family life to be congruent with this choice" (Hock et al. 1985: 400).

Interpersonal and contextual factors, such as the level of participation of husbands in family work, the amount of conflict perceived in marriages, and the general ease with which mothers can combine employment and parenting have also been found to be factors in women's decisions about employment (Desai and Waite 1991; Volling and Belsky 1993). Although the level of husbands' supportiveness is related to employed mothers' reports of their well-being (Gray et al. 1990), new mothers' feelings about their employment have not frequently been examined with reference to the social contexts in which they live. Yet, as Rosanna Hertz and Faith Ferguson (1995) point out, doing paid work carries with it the consequence that women who have grown up with the belief that mothers are irreplaceable must find a way of "replacing" themselves during the hours that they are away from home.

These are themes that appear in the commentary of the new parents I interviewed. There are constraints on the choices that new parents make in their approaches to employment and child care, particularly as a result of differentiation in how maternal and paternal accountability are conceptualized. This differentiation is institutionalized in economic structures and enters into various interactions that new parents have with each other, with work places, and with nonmaternal child care.

How Employment and Parenthood Fit

When I asked new parents what they thought society expected of mothers and fathers, many answered in terms of how parenting and employment were supposed to fit together. There was a sense among some parents that paid work might be in conflict with parenting:

> It seems like society is so screwed up, you know? I think a lot of people's priorities are screwed up. I mean I know that people have to work, but it just seems like it gets out of hand sometimes. (Melissa)

> I don't think parents take as much responsibility for their children as they should. Meaning maybe the mother and father work so they expect that the other one is going to do something and neither one does. So basically the child is on his own. (Bob)

The approach that parents took to evaluating the role of work in parenting was often explicitly gendered. In relation to mothers, the question was whether they should be employed, while for fathers it was how much child care they should do in light of being employed. Most people agreed that fathers *should* be employed while many perceived mothers as *allowed* to be employed, assuming that they took responsibility for things at home and were available for their child at all other times. Liza commented, "I think the reality of the situation is that most people have to work these days, most people do, whether it be that they want to, need to financially, or whatever. My idea of a good mother is somebody that gives their all to that child when they're there."

While a number of women argued that employment is now part of societal expectations for mothers — that it is part of "doing it all" — they had not necessarily revised their notions of what it means to be a good mother in the context of the added expectation that they be employed. That is, even though many mothers did paid work, many held onto the image of mothers as primary and indispensable to babies (see also McMahon 1995). The women I spoke with tended to differ from each other by how they perceived the consequences of their doing paid work, rather than by anything more specific about the nature of their work per se. While other research highlights important differences among women of different classes (see Burris 1991; Ferree 1987; McMahon 1995), there were no striking class differences in the benefits and conflicts from work experienced by the women I interviewed. This may be because, as Hays (1996) describes, mothers across classes and employment statuses share a commitment to the ideology of intensive mothering.

Among the men I interviewed, I found something different. This group of men did seem to be differentiated from each other, not by the fact of employment per se, but by what I loosely call here class differences. In particular, I refer to the conditions under which the fathers worked: what kind of work they did, how they were compensated, and how much control they felt they had over their work lives. Working-class fathers (roughly 40 percent of the men in my study) expressed more ambivalence about how their work shaped their images as fathers than middle- and upper-middle-class fathers did.

Those fathers who had professional/managerial-type jobs, particularly jobs in which they were well-paid and had a lot of flexibility in their schedules, appreciated these aspects of their jobs and did not experience much conflict between their paid work and fathering. To the extent that they did, it was in having difficulty pulling themselves away from their work. For these men, a sense of obligation to their wives and babies kept them from working longer hours:

> *Maddy is normally eager to have me home and some days she calls up and lets me know that she is eager to have me home, so that's been hard in a sense. (Phil)*

> *It was tough because my job allowed me to break away earlier but that left a lot of pressure on me to be the first one home and there were times when it was hard for me to break away, but I could, because I had no one to report to locally. (Chip)*

This was in contrast to men who were less in control of their work schedules, who were not on salaries, and who felt less prestige associated with their work. These men wanted jobs that would give them the opportunity to be in more control of their schedules and to either work less or different shifts:

> *I kind of feel that if I had a less stressful job and if I had a less physical job I'd have more energy like when I get home in the evening I'd have more energy to spend with him. (Todd)*

> *I want a normal type job where you work eight to five and you have your weekends off. I mean, when he grows up if he wants to play sports, when are all the games? They are going to be in the evenings or on weekends and I don't want to miss that. (Jay)*

One father, who was currently unemployed but who had had a series of different jobs, evaluated them based on their schedules. His last job, Eddie said, had been a good one because: "I went in after she went to the sitter and I got home a half hour after Sarah. So that was the best part about that job. That was perfect."

Financial security and benefits were also on some fathers' minds. Joel talked about having learned a trade: "But I'd like to find something more secure where also I could get some benefits for our family." Bill described his unhappiness with a boss who had not given him a break when his daughter was born, yet who he could not afford to alienate: "She was born and I went back to work the next day. Now how many guys do that? That felt really bad, you know, leaving my wife in the hospital overnight, although I did go to visit her early in the morning. And I had to go in that Saturday to finish a job up, you know, because being flat-rate, he controls your pay."

Although Bill said that he stayed in his job because it pays well and because he wants to be able to provide his daughter with "everything that she wants or everything that I can give her," he worried that she might be embarrassed by what he does as she gets older: "The things I wear, the work clothes, I don't look like anything important. I mean I make all right money, you know . . . Because you go over to the mall to eat and see these guys in their suits and stuff—I know I make more money than they do, but what am I supposed to do, wear a sign on my head that says that?"

For Bill, there was conflict in his job allowing him to be a good provider in terms of how he was compensated financially, but not necessarily giving him the appearance of being one. Jay also talked about the inadequacy of his job in terms of how he appears to others; here's how he described the job he'd like to get upon his discharge from the military: "A job where I could wear a suit, have a company car . . ."

"What does it mean to you to wear a suit?" I asked.

"Just a coat and tie, nice clothes. Have you seen dungarees?"

"I've seen dungarees, sure."

"You know the big bell-bottoms like, you know, Danny Partridge, Greg Brady, tight pants and you wear the same clothes as everybody—everybody matches. I view my job more as a blue collar, you know, type job and I want to be more of a white collar worker."

For Bill, there was an added irony in the physical risk he experienced because of the toxicity of the materials he works with: "Another thing that worries me is all the stuff I have to breathe in. I hope that doesn't shorten my life. Hopefully it won't. But I don't want her to be embarrassed by what I do, and if I could live a longer life." Trading off the negative health effects of this job for its financial benefits, Bill said that he holds onto the job out of his desire to provide well for his daughter: "I guess I'd probably get another job where I wouldn't have to breathe the stuff in, but because I'm making the money I'm making doing it, I'm going to stick with it just so I can give her everything, you know."

Although professional/managerial and working-class fathers differed in how they evaluated the fit between their jobs and parenthood, mothers across classes engaged in debate about whether they should be employed at all (see also Cowan and Cowan 1992). There were no clear patterns in the group of parents I interviewed in how family incomes interacted with the decisions about employment that couples made.

Belsky and Kelly (1994) note that the more attached a new mother is to the notion of work as a career, the more vulnerable she is to a drop in marital satisfaction after having a child. It makes sense that women who are more work-identified have greater adjustments to make in incorporating motherhood into their lives than women who are less identified with work. Some mothers expressed the sentiment that their jobs had become secondary to their husbands' jobs. Yet, among the women I met, marital satisfaction did not appear to depend on work status, in the sense that there were as many stay-at-home mothers who were irritated with their husbands as employed mothers.

The effect that work status appeared to have on some of the mothers was in the role work played in their construction of themselves as mothers. Mothers who were currently in the paid labor force had various levels of conflict (from virtually none to a lot), but even those on the high end of the conflict continuum did not entirely dismiss their need to work. Mothers who were no longer in the paid labor force rationalized in the opposite direction. For example, one stay-at-home mother, Ann Marie, said that she had planned on taking over a family business, but it had been sold. I asked her if she would be working now if it hadn't been sold, and she replied, "I don't know. I guess everything works out the way it's supposed to, you know what I mean? They sold it and then it was time for me to have a baby."

Mandy described her transformation from someone who needed her career to someone who was meant to be home: "It's so weird because in a way I felt like I needed the job and was afraid to give it up. I needed my career. But then you know in the same light I don't miss it at all. I just was meant to be home with him now. So it's just so strange because you're caught right in the middle. You think you need one thing but you really don't."

Whitney described all of the benefits of the job she had left to stay at home with her baby, yet concluded that she was "ready for a change": "I was the supervisor there and it was a good job and it was good paying, it had good benefits, it had good health insurance and that whole thing, all your holidays off, and I could go on and on. It was really good, and the people were good to work for. I was getting bored with it. I think I had done it for too long and I was ready for a change. I really was."

Factors related to jobs—availability, work conditions, and so forth—play a role in women's decisions about work, careers, and motherhood (Gerson 1985). For some of the women I interviewed, staying home with a baby was a way to justify leaving dissatisfying work:

> We had basically decided before she was born . . . because I wasn't enjoying my job, the feeling was, well, if I'm miserable at home and feel I need work, I would want another job anyway. (Maddy)

> It's different if you're doing something that you really love, you know, then a sacrifice would have been harder to make. But I didn't really consider it a sacrifice. (Gloria)

This appeared to be a more acceptable resolution for mothers than it was for a father who was similarly unhappy with his work. In discussing the possibility of relocating for a job his wife was applying for, Tom said, "I'll have time to rethink what we've got going. But also if I do that I'll feel really like a slug. I'll go, 'My God, you're just like, you're Samantha's housewife.'"

While Tom anticipated feeling "like a slug" if he were to be a househusband, some women saw raising a child as a contribution they could make in light of not having other ambitions anyway:

> *I've never had any big career that I really wanted to have that would have even been a big conflict with me, and I think raising a good human being, it takes time and effort and I'm willing to do that now. (Gloria)*

> *I don't want to work . . . My neighbor said something about how she had to figure out what she wanted to do for the rest of her life. She said, "You don't have to worry about that. You don't care about a career, do you?" (Ann Marie)*

And some, like Melissa, simply perceived taking care of a baby as a full-time job and as a mother's job: "I think this is the way it should be. I really do. This is my job. I just think if you're going to be a mom, then go all the way and do it." Jennifer Glass and Lisa Riley (1997) find that women with traditional beliefs are most likely to exit the labor force after becoming mothers.

Because of the expectation that mothers are home with their babies, or yearn to be home if they cannot be, some mothers emphasized the financial necessity of their employment and were somewhat self-conscious about wanting to be employed. Sarah said, "I'd like to be able to do things differently but unfortunately economics says that I can't do it that way." She then added, "And at the same time I didn't really think that I would want to stay home."

Peggy made the following admission, after saying that she'd have loved to stay home with her son "forever," but financially she couldn't: "Like some days actually I'm — this probably sounds bad — but some days I'm like — he [child] is very active now and I'm happy to go to work because it is a break." She then went on to label herself as selfish because she was employed even though her family might not be completely poor if she wasn't: "I mean I could probably not work and we could just make ends meet, but I don't want to live with that strain right now . . . I mean I know there is money in the bank and I know I have a check coming and I don't feel nervous about taking care of him or his needs. I like it that way. I don't want to feel, you know, like we are living check to check . . . I mean it is kind of selfish but that's the big reason I'm working now."

"Why do you say it's selfish?" I asked.

"Because like I said, if I wasn't, I might have been here all the time for him."

Peggy's view that she should be "here all the time" for her son meant that working was something she was doing against her son's best interests. It was not unusual for the employed women I met to see their employment as in conflict with their babies' best interests. Ironically, research findings suggest that the opposite may be the case over time: Mothers who are happily employed are the least depressed group of mothers in the country; conversely, mothers who are not employed are more likely to be depressed and to provide poor mothering for their children (Scarr 1990).

Some of the mothers I met were clear about the benefits of employment for themselves, focusing in particular on social networks:

I enjoy getting out of the house . . . it's a very social thing for me. And yet it's my job, my career. (Liza)

I like what I do and I think it's good to have your own identity. It's good to be able, you know, like I said, work is therapy. I mean I do see my friends there. (Harriet)

I'm a working kind of person. I mean I do get enjoyment out of having a nice home, but I just can't mop and vacuum.

> *I need to do something else. Just to keep my mind busy. Just*
> *to have someone to talk to. (Laura)*

A couple of women talked about their workplaces being their major sources of support during their pregnancies, and Laura, who travels a distance to her job, expressed loss about not being able to hang around with people after work anymore.

Others were more explicit about how their home life was enhanced by their employment:

> *I don't feel a conflict at all. I am a much better person,*
> *I think, working. I focus when I'm working and when I'm*
> *at home. I think I'd lose my bananas if I was home all the*
> *time. (Ruth)*

> *I feel a lot more fulfilled than I would if I were home five*
> *days a week. I think the time that I do spend with her is*
> *much more quality time than if I were home all the time.*
> *(Morgan)*

Eileen suggested that the quality of her work had been improved by her becoming a mother — that she was more herself and that it was paying off for her professionally: "I think in some ways I'm a lot more me professionally than I used to be . . . I think it's maybe given me a sense of freedom. I'm a lot more blunt than I might be. And ironically it might be why I'm doing much better because I'm a lot more creative. I'm more willing to do things that if I was really focused on being promoted by the end of the year, I wouldn't take some of the risks I've taken."

How do these kinds of statements jibe with the tendency of new mothers to worry more and to not feel like they are living up to images for mothers? I think for many mothers these internal conflicts are the prices they pay for their jobs. Their jobs per se are generally not problematic and may even support the quality of their mothering when they're home. But the stress comes from negotiating their desires to see themselves as good mothers and good workers at the same time (see Glass and Estes [1997] on the encroachment of "industrial" time on family time). Even though Eileen's work had improved, she nevertheless worried that she was spending too much time at it; and other mothers, like Morgan, described their worries about moving in and out of motherhood: "That's the hardest thing for me, I think, was trying to do a good job at work and also be a good mother and keep up with everything around the house and stuff too."

Some mothers imagined that working part-time would be less stressful, and there does seem to be less turnover in jobs that allow mothers to reduce hours (Glass and Riley 1997). Harriet explained, "I mean if I worked three or four days a week I would be happy, I really would. I mean I think that would be enough time out of the house that you would feel like you had your own identity and at the same time you'd have enough time to spend with your family that, you know, it would be complete."

Mothers who worked part-time *did* present themselves as feeling less stress, as Maddy did: "I think to work full-time, it would be very difficult for me. I think I would resent work and have a lot of guilt. But what I'm doing now, and working part-time, I'm able to keep them very separate." Yet Sylvia, who declared herself to have "a great balance" in working three days per week, said, "What I have the hardest time dealing with is sort of renegotiating my identity." Working part-time did not necessarily protect mothers from dealing with the tensions involved in acknowledging what they got from their jobs: money that their families needed, work that was challenging, coworkers who provided social stimulation, and time *away* from their children.

COUPLES' INTERACTIONS AROUND EMPLOYMENT

The image of mothers being essential to babies was often expressed in couples' decisions about how they would change their employment upon the birth of their babies. Several fathers expressed the belief that it was better for their child for them to carry the employment load and for their wives to be more available to their child:

> *If there is a choice, I would want to be the one to be putting in more work and let her spend the time with the baby. (David)*

> *If it was going to be one of us [spending time with the baby], I would want it to be her, to be Andrea . . . because she is the mother and . . . that's just kind of the way it's supposed to be. (Wade)*

Mothers often agreed that it is their job to take primary responsibility for the care of their babies. And some new mothers were explicit about their belief that their children were better off with them than with their fathers. Margaret said, for example, "I cook and clean up and stuff and David is sort of, I don't know, like, give him [child] chocolate chip cookies and, you know, Coke or something."

Some fathers whose wives were at home full-time perceived the care their wives gave their babies as ensuring that they could do their job as providers:

> *I'm not paid great but I'm paid enough that Melissa doesn't have to work and at the same time by Melissa being at home I have the flexibility to deal with the problems at work and not have to find a baby-sitter. (Brett)*

> *Her being home with the baby, I don't have any doubts that she's doing the right things. So I'll go along thinking that because of that, I can still put my attention to my work and be able to do a good job and think about the future and be a success so I can do a good job supporting them. (Wade)*

The husband just quoted was a thirty-two-year-old, white, middle-class man who had gone through a period of unemployment, but had found a job necessitating a relocation for him and his wife and child. I met them just before their move. Wade was commuting and Andrea was home with their child, something about which she made positive statements followed by less positive ones: "I like being home a lot. I really do. I'm a real organized type person so sometimes I get really frustrated because I feel like it's taking me all day to get dressed and do a couple of loads of laundry. . . . I think work would probably be more of a chore for me because I would really want to be with Jessica. I mean I love it when she goes down for her nap some days or with Wade away most of the week, sometimes I really look forward to eight or 8:30 when you're going to bed."

During the time Wade was unemployed, Andrea went to work: "I liked going out in the morning and he took care of the baby and coming home and he had dinner ready and I really liked that. I liked having something to do and having others waiting for me and waiting on me. I liked that. But then when it ended, I was also glad to be back home with Jessica."

The ambivalence in Andrea's statements suggested an accountability to the image of mothers wanting nothing more than to be home with their children. Yet she was also sensitive to other people's responses to her being at home and described interactions with other women in particular, whom she characterized as "jealous." Wade also mentioned women putting pressure on each other: "I think there's a lot of pressure on women in general to be successful, to be career-type people . . . A lot of women really think they have to compete with the men and they want to be on an even keel all the time, which is great if they can do it."

Although Wade said that he thought it was great for women to be on an even keel with men, it was clear that his own approach was that Andrea and he had different jobs to do in their family. Andrea also suggested that her being employed might have negative effects on their joint construction of family: "You have that money left over and what do you do? You buy Chinese, you buy pizza, because you're not up to cooking. And he's the type who likes to come home. He doesn't mind if dinner is not on the table but he likes to come home and have a nice family meal and that's kind of how we both grew up. Dinner was real important."

Another mother who had left the labor market, Mandy, suggested that women could trade off earning income for ensuring that they were available to their children and that family was their highest priority: "Family is most important and now we are doing it on one income. Now, you know, we have the luxury of being able to say okay, when I go back to work, I don't have to get that $30,000 or $40,000 a year job that I may have been in line for before. I can take an $18,000 a year job or a $15,000 or whatever and do something fun and do something that I like and that will work around our children."

Like Andrea, Mandy expressed sensitivity to other people's judgments of her work status: "I think at first I didn't want to give up the responsibility of having my own job and telling people I worked." Mandy's husband, Chip, understood her feelings about being perceived as unproductive, arguing that there should be tangible compensations for staying home with a child: "If you had to put a price on it, I'm sure it would be well above $50,000 . . . There should be tax advantages." But, he went on, "There's nobody to lobby for the wives."

The comments of Mandy's that follow suggest that she could no longer advocate for herself in the context of her life with Chip because she had lost her leverage in no longer having a job. But, she concluded, this was okay: "It's funny now because he is the breadwinner so there have been opportunities where he has interviewed for positions, had opportunities to relocate and get a better position and the money was better. You're just put in a position where you have to just follow. Before, when we were both working, we would talk it out. I'd say, 'No I want to stay here.' And now you really can't. I just feel like I would have to go and probably we as a family follow Chip's career path, and I would gladly do it."

While being employed full-time was a trade-off in terms of women's conformance with the good mother image, unemployment also carried trade-offs for women in marital power. Griswold

(1993: 3) argues that men's historical monopoly on breadwinning has allowed them to leave "the boring, repetitious, and vexing work of child care to their wives . . . Even today, most men resist the onerous tasks of child care because it is in their interest to do so." Women I interviewed did not necessarily identify this trade-off, however. Rather, as Mandy did, they framed their behavior in the interest of prioritizing family. Mandy "gladly" lost her bargaining power in order to comply with constructions of good mothering and family. Harriet, on the other hand, "bought" her way out of them. She worked relatively long hours, and her husband, Arnie, tended to spend more time with their daughter. He said of Harriet's employment: "I have no problem with that and she makes the bigger bucks, so I say more power to her."

Couples who needed or enjoyed the benefits of two incomes had varying ways of dealing with this fact, and here the diversity of imagery, and the supermom image in particular, came in handy. In some couples, for example, the mother's employment was absorbed into their images of motherhood and fatherhood, as long as the mother remained the primary parent. Jake, who described his family arrangements as traditional, said of his and Ruth's division of labor: "We both have similar types of jobs in that we . . . travel quite a bit, so if one is away, the other has to do all those tasks that need to be done. Feed him, bathe him, hold him, change him, everything." Jake added that Ruth has a closer relationship with their son "naturally because she is the mother"; she "probably does a little more because he is more drawn to her."

Ruth also did not see her work as interfering with her image of a good mother. Comparing herself to her mother, she said, "My mother didn't work, she was home after school, she drove all the car pools, and she chaperoned all the field trips. I think she was a wonderful mother and I hope to be able to do the same type of thing. I'll probably be working but always hopefully in a job flexible enough to drive the car pools or to do whatever."

In other cases, there was more ambivalence about how maternal employment fit into the picture, and people struggled with the desire for the extra income and the sense that it was better for a mother to be at home. Todd, a twenty-six-year-old white father, worked in a mill that was very erratic in assigning shifts. He didn't like the idea of his wife being employed, but he referred to his wife's job as a blessing because she "has a say in what [shifts] she works": "Don't consider me like a male chauvinist pig but I don't believe that she should work if she don't want. I don't want her to work. I wish she could spend all of the time in the world with Jerry. But she feels the need to work. I feel the need that she has to work. So she is doing it until the time that she can quit."

Bill said that he thought having a mother at home was "a plus," but he did want his wife to bring in more income eventually: "Later on I'd like to see her get a different job." I asked him what kind of job, and he said, "Just something that pays a little bit more. And if she could get a job with really good benefits, because my benefits are expensive, you know, where it could kind of ease the burden on my paycheck, that would be good too. Just something to bring more money into the house."

Bill wanted a different home than the trailer in which they were living, which fueled his interest in his wife working more. For him, having a house was part of being a family: "Because I kind of like being a family, you know. I mean this isn't a house, but trying to save for one. Doing things like this, doing the lawn and stuff, I don't know, I just like doing stuff . . . I gotta get better curtains than what's up there, but that's stuff I like to do." Having the ability to buy a home, one of the dominant images of family, might justify a mother's employment, as in Stuart's case: "If we didn't [both work] we probably wouldn't be living in this house right now." In the case of Ashley and Bill, however, Ashley was less concerned about getting a house than she was with how available she would be to their child if she got a full-time job: "He says that we'd be able to afford a house if I had a full-time job. But when she has vacations in school and if she gets off the bus at three and I'm stuck at work until five, I don't want that."

Ken acknowledged the need for his wife to be employed, but he thought that Morgan placed too much priority on her job: "Sometimes my perception is that she'd rather stay here [at work] because it's a little easier." Despite Ken's displeasure with Morgan's commitment to her work, he could not rationalize the loss of her salary if she stopped. I asked him if he would like it if she was willing to stop working, and he replied, "We talked about that, but when you look at what she makes, that's the big difference. Right away I'd say yes, but then we try to figure out our finances, going from what she makes to zero, forget it. At one point we were thinking for what we pay in taxes, she's better off not working, taxes and day care and all that. A lot of people say that, but when you really put that on paper, that's bullshit. Two bucks an hour for baby-sitting and whatever, it doesn't come close to a decent salary."

The cost-benefit analysis that Ken performed of paying a baby-sitter versus his wife's salary was one that has been documented in other research. Rather than seeing child care as a cost that they have as a couple, it is not unusual for people to focus on the woman's employment specifically (see Cowan and Cowan 1992). Liza, a mother in the highest family-income category in the group of parents I interviewed said, for example, "On my salary, if we were to have another child, I really can't afford to have two in day care."

Among the issues considered was not only how much would be left over in the paycheck after paying for child care, but if that amount was worth not conforming to the mother-at-home ideal. Bob said, "Baby-sitting is pretty expensive if she works full-time. So it's more beneficial for both Donna and for us for her to stay home."

Andrea described the interaction between her lower paying job and Wade's wishes: "Working in human services, I never really made enough money to make it really worthwhile to pay for the baby-sitting and to be out of the house. . . . He wanted me home, he just doesn't want other people raising his children."

When there were any concerns about a child's adjustments or how couples were constructing themselves as a family, mothers' outside work tended to be implicated. Gil said, for example: "We saw changes in Carrie when Miranda started going to school and stuff, because she just wasn't getting the attention that she was before." Chip said of Mandy, who started a night job after spending the day with their baby, "I hate to sound like a whiner but it was hard when you came home. I didn't get a chance to see Mandy. We were always in a transition period. Robbie never got to see us together. That's important to see everybody together."

There were several couples who agreed that wives' part-time employment worked well. Part-time employment seemed to pose less of a challenge to the notion that a mother should be primary and present. Ashley said of her part-time work, "I wanted to spend most of my time with her. I haven't missed anything either. First steps, nothing."

Bob's use of the pronoun "we" in the following comments reflects the joint construction of parenting arrangements: "I like the way Whitney's schedule is. It gets her out of the house every now and then, but it keeps her home long enough that we're raising Donna, not somebody else." Whitney's presence in particular meant that they—and not someone else—were raising their child.

It appeared also that part-time work did not interfere with some couples' notions that the wife's employment was optional. Phil said of his wife's part-time job, "I think it's been ideal. She seems to enjoy getting out of the house." Maddy agreed that the job had been useful for getting her out of the house: "By Friday afternoon, having been with the baby all week, I was so eager for Phil to get home, and he would come home at 6:15 when I expected him at six, and I'd say, 'You're late!' Whereas the weeks I worked, it got me out just enough." Yet later Phil commented that if Maddy wasn't working, they'd be spending more money than they were taking in. Her income literally kept them from going into debt, but both Maddy and Phil had framed Maddy's job as if it were an extracurricular activity.

Perhaps it does not matter how husbands and wives conceptualize maternal employment as long as everyone is happy. But it could matter much more if everyone does not stay happy. Couples made decisions as if they were a team, but only one of the players was damaged by the possible long-term implications of changing their job trajectories. Labor force interruptions are detrimental for women's long-term occupational attainment (Glass and Riley 1997) and part-time employment plays a role in the lower wages of women with children (Waldfogel 1997). Women who change jobs after having babies, in order to maximize their financial and family accommodations, get less improvement than they might have because of their weak market position (Estes and Glass 1996). The lack of gender equity in the labor market results in difficulties for mothers both in maintaining availability to their children and economic stability at the same time. With a national divorce rate of 50 percent, for new mothers to make choices that minimize their job stability and earning power might be treacherous indeed (see Arendell 1986). But with the pressure on mothers to be present for their babies, there is no one watching out for mothers' long-term interests.

In her analysis of feeding, DeVault (1991: 154–156) notes that women who do not do all the work "risk the charge—not only from others, but in their own minds as well—that they do not care about the family." DeVault points out that in the family context, "a mother's claims for time to pursue her own projects can so easily be framed as a lack of care, and a mother's claim to be 'a person' may be taken as 'selfish.'" This analysis is relevant to understanding how women do not always recognize that their own interests may not be served by choices that they make in the interest of their family.

Maddy was one mother who recognized that she might be sacrificing future earnings unnecessarily: "I can be short-sighted so I could definitely sabotage myself here, but I think that I would be very happy continuing to work part-time . . . Being hourly rather than salary is less, but it doesn't bother me. But come back in fifteen years, maybe I'll say, 'Oh gee, I could be doing something to be making more money and it wouldn't have hurt her at all.'" It is telling that Maddy framed her change in work schedule and pay as an attempt not to "hurt" her daughter. The notion that children are harmed if cared for by anyone other than their mothers influences new parents' experiences with nonparental care.

Who is Raising the Children?

As with other baby-related mental labor, mothers I interviewed tended to take particular responsibility for finding, interacting with, and worrying about child care providers:

> I've got this week covered, but I don't even know who's watching him next week. (Maggie)

> It was really tough. I looked a long time to find licensed day care . . . She's actually not licensed, but I'm very happy with her . . . I had to go through two people first before ending up with her. (Barbara)

How the parents I interviewed perceived nonparental child care was an important element in how they conceptualized a mother being employed. For some women, discomfort with the idea of day care was the factor that pulled them out of the work force, as Mandy said, " I just thought, 'This is it. Now it is facing us. Do we put him in day care and just keep doing this, or do we stay home?' And the answer wasn't a big decision, and we just decided that I would stay home with him."

Whitney told of her decision to leave her job: "I had worked in a [job] for about eight years and it took me a long time to get where I was . . . When I had her we both decided that it would be best if I stayed home, at least for the first six months or so."

"What went into that decision for you?" I asked.

"Well, child care was a big problem for us. You know, being in the Navy, you move around a lot and I knew a lot of the wives in the area that did child care, but they had five or six other kids and she just wouldn't get that attention that she would, of course, get from her mother. And we both just decided that it would be best. So we gave up a lot, we did give up a lot."

Whitney had been in child care and had negative memories of it, but ultimately her position was shaped not so much by her concerns about child care as by her belief that children are happier if their mothers, in particular, are home (Hertz and Ferguson [1995: 2] also find that decisions about child care are embedded in these kinds of "implicit family sentiments"): "I think I missed that a lot, having my mother home, because my father, I mean he was really good with us, he was very good with us, but, you know, you always like to have your mommy home."

Couples in which the mothers were staying at home often expressed very consistent concerns about child care—images of neglect and abuse highlighted in the media. Elliot and Nancy, both twenty-two years old, lived on Elliot's wages from restaurant work. He said: "I couldn't feel more comfortable with anyone but her own mom watching her, especially the way things are these days." Nancy agreed, "It's just my big fear of this sickness that goes on with these adults and it just happens so much and you don't know when it's gonna happen and the only way you can be sure is if it's you that's watching them, you know?" Perhaps ironically, Nancy planned to become a paid child care provider in the future.

Other fathers whose wives or partners were at home also mentioned concerns about the kind of care their children would get from someone other than their own mother:

> *You're constantly hearing on the news about kids getting molested or beat or things like that by baby-sitters. (Gil)*

> *I've seen, you know, you see the 60 Minutes when they did the day care . . . a child will sit in a dirty diaper for eight hours a day and then right before the parents come they change the diaper real quick. (Jay)*

Jay suggested that children will inevitably be less well cared for by someone other than their own parent/mother: "My child is important to me. Another child, well, it's not less, or I wouldn't, how do I say this? I wouldn't ignore that child, you know, but it is not going to mean as much as Dylan means. If you're watching my child, I'm not saying you would neglect my child, but if it was your own child, you would definitely pay more attention and if he was crying you would jump. If another person's child was crying you might let them cry for a minute longer or something." He suggested that Gloria would provide Dylan with more help: "She can help him in his development years playing with his toys or whatever. You put them in a day care and they don't get that."

Wade described himself and Andrea as "not big on the idea of day care": "Before we had the baby we really decided we wanted her to be home with the baby just because it would mean that much more for us to be the ones — her mostly — who is doing the teaching, who's rearing the child." Andrea concurred that she and Wade were "not big believers in day care." She attributed the illnesses and misbehavior of friends' children to their being in day care: "We have friends whose children are in day care and always sick and at four months old had the chicken pox and at two years old came to our house once and could talk up a storm, tapping his mom on the shoulder, 'Mommy may I please interrupt I have something to say?' but on the other hand, he was on top of the couch and climbing all over the furniture."

The phrase "I don't want someone else raising my child" was used repeatedly by parents I interviewed, and some of the mothers in dual-earner couples were especially troubled by this concept. Eileen mentioned Jimmy's relationship with his child care provider as a barometer for his relationship with her, saying that it would "kill" her if she someday arrived to fetch him and he didn't want to leave (which frequently happens, particularly with toddlers in child care). The rivalry that Eileen felt with "the other woman" in her baby's life was a feeling that people expected from mothers. Harriet said of her daughter's baby-sitter: "I feel very very comfortable with her and I don't ever feel jealous. Some are like, 'Well don't you feel jealous when you see [child] hug her or kiss her?' And no, I mean I feel comfortable knowing that my daughter is that comfortable with her."

Sean suggested that Sylvia's discomfort with their child care provider had something to do with female competition: "It's harder for Sylvia, and I see it as the fact that she is a woman and this is another woman who is taking care of the kid." What Sylvia described was an uneasiness with their child care provider's reports about their son Brian: "We've tried to decide whether she's just reporting or complaining . . . I get nervous like he's bothering the other babies . . . A lot of that's me, a lot of it's pressure that I put on myself. I don't know why I do it. But day care has been hard for me . . . I go back and forth thinking sometimes I'm so stressed out about day care, would it be better if I stay home? And I ultimately come to the conclusion, no. Because I think that day care is really good for Brian."

Sylvia's anxiety about child care led her to consider leaving her job, and as we've seen, other mothers cut back on parts of their jobs or left them completely so that their children would not spend long hours with baby-sitters. In this way, the parents I interviewed conformed with findings from other research that a majority of mothers consider parental care to be the ideal form of care for preschool age children (Mason and Kuhlthau 1989). What quantitative analyses do not necessarily reveal is the role of child care providers themselves in reinforcing some mothers' worries, as in Eileen's case: "We have a sitter who is a wonderful sitter and every so often she will say something—she doesn't have a mean bone in her body—but it's just kind of directed about the way that she raised her kids. I don't know if she ever had a career. She was home, you know, she was home all the time. And how I'm not doing it. And that cuts pretty deep."

Gloria is a thirty-one-year-old, working-class, white woman, who described herself as a "house frau" with no career aspirations. She is married to Jay, a thirty-year-old white man, who was hoping to find an upwardly mobile job following a stint in the military. Gloria got paid by a friend to baby-sit and described herself making the kind of judgments that mothers feared: "You wouldn't get a dog if you couldn't come in and let it out a couple of times in a ten-hour period, but people are having children. And like I was telling [friend], 'You wouldn't give me your car to drive for the weekend but I have your baby for forty-five hours every week.'" Although she was invoking guilt in her friend, Gloria then went on to characterize her friend as doing "a lot of guilt stuff which makes it hard" on her child.

As a baby-sitter, Gloria participated in the kind of no-win interactions some of the other mothers in the sample described having with their child care providers. She also described the devaluation that perhaps plays a role in shaping the relationships between mothers and the women who help to care for their children: "These people that take care of our children. The lowest paid, people have hardly any respect, but we're putting our children's lives in their hands. I don't think I would shout around, 'Oh yeah, I'm a baby-sitter.'"

"Because you don't think that would impress anyone?" I asked.

"No I don't. It doesn't impress me."

"It doesn't impress you?"

"No. But it has worked out great for me though. I mean, that's our grocery budget, and I don't have to leave my child for a second," she replied.

In not leaving her child "for a second," Gloria achieved the presence she felt was required of a good mother, and her own experience of baby-sitting reinforced her view that good mothers don't leave their children with anyone else. She described the things she does for her friend's daughter as "less automatic" and said that it was a good thing that the child sleeps a lot because she was not going to "slight" her own child while taking responsibility for someone else's.

Most of the employed parents that I interviewed used some form of family day care — care provided in the home of a child care provider. This is the type of care used by a majority of parents of infants and toddlers nationally (Kahn and Kamerman, cited in Rapp and Lloyd 1989). While there is research suggesting that the choice of family day care over center-based care reflects ideological differences between mothers (Rapp and Lloyd 1989), I think that Margaret Nelson (1994: 181) is correct in suggesting that "it is not surprising that many women seek a form of substitute care resembling that which some mothers used to, and most women are expected to, offer their own children." Couples look for care that approximates a traditional family, according to Hertz (1986: 153), who suggests that they "equate quality with intensity and one-on-one care, believing this to be the best substitute for the traditional mother." Turning to center-based care may be an acknowledgment that a baby will get something different during those hours than they would have at home.

Nelson's study of more than three hundred family day care providers supports my contentions that family day care providers may reinforce, rather than relieve, maternal guilt about employment. She suggests that many family day care providers are motivated to be at-home providers so that they can be home with their own children. They are therefore providing a service that facilitates "the movement of other women into the labor force even though they fervently believe these women should remain at home" (Nelson 1994: 192; see, however, Fitz Gibbon [1995] for a discussion of the development of feminist consciousness in some family day care providers).

The lack of support that mothers feel from their child care providers may be something that is difficult to acknowledge to themselves or the provider ("she doesn't have a mean bone in her body," Eileen said), because of new mothers' vulnerability and concerns about alienating the person who is taking care of their baby. Sylvia was not always sure about how to interpret reports that she got about her baby Brian from her family day care provider, Judy. Instead of criticizing Judy for complaining about Brian, Sylvia worried that Brian would cause Judy problems: "She's quite a wonderful person and they are quite a wonderful little family . . . I worry a lot about is Brian going to be okay, is he going to be fussy a lot with Judy today?"

In trying to explain her discomfort, Sylvia was careful to say that she was not questioning Judy as a person or whether Brian was getting proper care. Yet it was clear that on some level Sylvia felt that her baby was not being understood by Judy:

*I'm always sort of feeling like he's just a little different than
other kids and I've tried to explain to Sean that I think she's
a new day care provider, she's brought up her own three children and she's at home and she has three really nice boys
and I like her relationship with them and her husband is a
real nice guy, but she has never done real day care before
and so I think that this is also a new thing for her. She may
have brought up three kids, but her own kids never went
through separation anxiety because they were always with
her, and one of the other babies she has doesn't go through
it, but Brian does. Some babies do and some don't.*

The fact that Sylvia felt that Judy did not understand separation anxiety and treated it as an inconvenience was a sign that
both she and Brian were probably not getting the support they
needed from Judy. Even more striking is that Sylvia and Judy both
believed that only babies whose mothers are employed experience separation anxiety, when, in fact, it is a normal developmental milestone that babies may experience regardless of whether
their mothers are employed or not.

The use of family day care by parents of preschool children
has decreased over the past few years while center-based programs
have seen the largest increases. Glass and Estes (1997) suggest that
in the same way that growth in female labor force participation
increases the demand for child care, it also decreases the supply,
since potential child care providers derive more financial benefits
in other parts of the labor market. I wonder also whether parents
have reacted to interactions like those I have described in this
chapter, as well as to media coverage of child care fiascoes, by
looking for child care that is more public, accountable, and de-
pendable — care in which children attach to the place as well as
to the people. Parents may be finding that their children have
greater continuity in center-based care and that there are positive differences between their own homes and centers in which
they find providers who are professionally invested in supporting
families.

I ran into Sylvia several months after I interviewed her and she picked up the discussion of her child care situation as if we had just paused for breath. Just that day, she had received a call from Judy at work that convinced her that she should no longer keep Brian in Judy's care. It had taken Sylvia months of worrying about her own and Brian's behavior to come to the realization that this was not a good match. As much as the parents who did not want to have their babies in the care of someone else speculated that baby-sitters are generally indifferent, neglectful, and perhaps abusive, it had been very difficult for Sylvia to allow herself to recognize her dissatisfaction with Judy. As one of the earlier quotes above indicated, she may not have been able to acknowledge her unhappiness with the situation because she perceived it as an indictment of her employment status and her belief that "day care is really good for Brian."

Sylvia also had little help from her husband in validating her discomfort with this specific situation and relationship. Sean had interpreted Sylvia's feelings as rivalry with another woman and dismissed Sylvia's perceptions that Judy complained about Brian: "Sean feels from the times that he's seen her and from my reporting of the conversation back that she's probably just sort of describing, you know, how the day has been." It had been Sylvia's job to carry the worry about Brian's child care, and it was now her decision to move on. I happened to run into her on the day she made this decision, before she had actually embarked on the potentially difficult search for a new child care provider. But for this moment, Sylvia seemed relieved, and even elated, to realize that perhaps she, Brian, and even day care itself had not been the problem.

Sandra Scarr, Deborah Phillips, and Kathleen McCartney (1989) suggest that the lack of coherent and national child care policy in the United States is a reflection of "cherished beliefs" related to maternal care: that mothers (as opposed to fathers or society) are individually responsible for the care of children, that at-home mothers provide the best care, and that there are no positive benefits for children from nonparental care. "Child care" versus "home care" is often debated without a recognition of the variations in quality that may appear in each and the mediating variables that may affect this quality. Fears related to child care are generated less by scientifically demonstrated facts than by notions about the obligations mothers have to children and the form these obligations should take (Scarr et al. 1989; see also Coontz 1992). The result is that mothers' need and enjoyment of employment poses a challenge to their images as good mothers with which both they and their husbands struggle.

The effects of both gender socialization and stratification were evident in the directions women's employment paths took upon becoming mothers. Some of the new mothers I met made decisions to leave good jobs based on their belief that this was best for their babies. They traded off financial and social benefits, as well as upward mobility, in order to be physically present to their babies. Others left lousy jobs—jobs that were significantly lower paying than their male partners'. While these mothers may have felt the need to leave their paid work in any case, the labor market did not give them many reasons to stay, and their pay scales did not provide much leverage for pushing their male partners to stay home had they been inclined to do so. Chip said, when we were talking about Mandy having left her job, "I kind of lucked out because I make more." Sylvia said that it had not been an option for Sean to change his hours as she had: "I mean he is making more money." In this sense, there seemed to be an intersection of images and structural arrangements that maintained, and even invited, a gendered division of baby care and economic provision.

CHAPTER 8

❧

Conclusion

TWO YEARS AFTER OUR INITIAL INTERVIEW, I MET with Eileen and Brendan to see how they were doing and to talk with them about my findings. They described stresses in their household, and they were expecting a second child. We talked about the models for mothers and fathers that Eileen had described in our first meeting, and she suggested that "a very big problem" they have is that she tries to apply to Brendan the same standards for his parenting that she applies to herself: "I have these stupid standards I have to live up to and I can't. So I have my own frustrations with that, and in the meantime, I apply that to him and he doesn't buy into it." Brendan agreed that the way they thought about good parenting differed: "I think that I'm a pretty good father and I think that I'm always there for Jimmy, but that doesn't mean I have to be physically always there."

The difference in what it meant to each of them to be "there" for their child was a source of tension both within Eileen and in her marriage to Brendan. While he saw his life as having come together, Brendan described Eileen's life as falling apart. Eileen did not disagree: "I'm feeling crowded a lot, trying to do the good mother thing, which takes priority, and trying to do the good [employee] thing, which has become bigger than I want it to be, and also the good wife thing . . . I mean, you get all three models going, and Brendan would say it's me, but it's probably more of a sociological thing than just me."

Eileen's point has been made throughout this book. But what I haven't said enough is that there is nothing inevitable about how women and men negotiate parenthood and that relationships and institutions can change.

OVERVIEW OF FINDINGS AND THEORETICAL IMPLICATIONS

This book highlights that gender differentiation in new parents is not only behavioral, but also reflects differences in what I have called "parental consciousness." While the tendency for mothers to feel ultimately responsible for babies has been identified in other studies of mothers (see, for example, McMahon 1995), this book has also described the content of fathers' consciousness and placed the parental consciousness of both parents in a relational and structural context. I have suggested that differences in how parenthood tends to occupy men and women internally are linked to social constructions of "good" mothering and fathering. That is, new mothers and fathers negotiate their parental roles in the context of socially constructed images of motherhood and fatherhood.

This study empirically establishes new parents' awareness of, and responses to, cultural imagery, and I have argued that this imagery is an underrecognized influence on their transitions into parenthood. Men and women have different transitions into parenthood as individuals and as couples, in part, because they are expected to and they are accountable to these expectations (see West and Fenstermaker 1993). The ways that men and women approach new parenthood together is a form of "doing gender": reproducing themselves as socially defined mothers and fathers and as socially defined women and men (West and Zimmerman 1987). Men and women who become parents together "do parenthood" together, and the way that mothers "mother" is influenced by fathers, as well as the other way around. While some of the parents I interviewed perceived changes in what is expected of mothers and fathers today, I argued that the more latent imagery they carried of good mothers and fathers has not necessarily been revised from a split between maternal nurturance and availability to babies and paternal economic provision and relative absence. Couples participated in reproducing these images. The mothers I interviewed tended to perceive more stereotypical expectations for fathers than fathers themselves did; and fathers perceived more stereotypical expectations for mothers than mothers did.[1] In cases in which fathers were employed and mothers were not, their arrangement literally depended on this accountability. But even in cases in which couples' behavior did not completely correspond to traditional expectations, the content of their thinking did. Differences in parental consciousness maintained a dichotomy between mothering and fathering — even in situations in which the women were employed and the men provided substantial physical baby care.

I also suggested that the interactions of couples reflect not only an adherence to images of "good" mothering and fathering, but also to more latent images of "good" wives and husbands. While the people I interviewed acknowledged differences in social expectations for mothers and fathers, they were less apt (men in particular) to suggest that wives have particular duties in marriages that husbands do not. Nevertheless, I presented data that illustrated the tendency for some wives to feel obliged to accommodate and defer to their husbands, although they did not necessarily acknowledge this dynamic (see also DeVault 1991). In addition, my interviews suggested that new parenthood has a tendency to skew even further imbalances already embedded in marriage as an institution because of changes in mothers' earnings as well as their dependence on their husbands for relief from their ongoing responsibility for babies (see LaRossa and LaRossa 1989).

This research suggests, therefore, that there is both a relational and an institutional context for gendered transitions into parenthood; these contexts exist within, and extend beyond, the relationships of individual couples. In their routine, daily interactions with each other and with other people, as well as in their encounters with social structures and institutions, new parents are channeled in the direction of experiencing motherhood and fatherhood as different from one another. This book has presented how interactional and institutional forms of reinforcement for gender differentiation are rooted in interpretations of mothers' and fathers' biological differences, in their experiences with families, and in the paid labor market. On both an interactional and an institutional level, differentiation between mothers and fathers reproduces gender as an identity, as a cultural symbol, and as a social structure (see Osmond and Thorne 1993).

One context for the reproduction of gender is the meaning that new parents and others ascribe to their physiological differences — to the fact that women experience pregnancy and have the capacity to breast-feed. I suggested that implicit in "advice" about feeding babies is an ideological construction of babies as constantly needing their mothers while their fathers are treated as peripheral. While other researchers have suggested that men are pushed out of caregiving by individual mothers (see Cowan and Cowan 1992), I have argued that interactions between mothers and fathers are, in part, determined by new parents' interpretations of messages they receive from baby care experts.

This book has also explored how men's and women's approaches to constructing themselves as fathers and mothers are influenced by their current interactions with family members, their interpretations of past family experiences, and institutional constructions of images of "the family." These interpretations are often linked to differentiation between caregiving and other forms of work.

Divisions of baby care between new fathers and mothers mirror the separation of "men's work" and "women's work" that not only structures families and households, but the economy as a whole. Segregation and differential pay within occupations, which reflect the institutionalization of gender difference, constrain the ability of some new parents to stray from traditional divisions of baby care. Mothers and fathers also participate in undermining women's economic power because of their accountability to the notion that mothers must "always be there" for their children. Ambivalence about maternal employment is apparent in attitudes about nonparental child care, which is conceptualized as replacing the mother in particular. Mothers are accountable to the image of worrying about their children when they are not with them (whether they actually are worried or not), which is an essential feature of differences in parental consciousness between mothers and fathers.

The result of these various forms of reinforcement of gender differentiation is that men and women as individuals, and as partners, have a difficult time going against the construction of mothers as ultimately responsible for babies and fathers as more peripheral to them. In this sense, individual parents may participate in reproducing gendered transitions into parenthood, but neither their behavior nor their consciousness can be conceptualized as separate from the imagery that is continuously reproduced in the interactions, structures, and institutions in which their lives are embedded.

Clinical and Policy Implications

In more than twenty longitudinal studies in different locations within the United States and overseas, transitions into parenthood have been found to negatively affect significant proportions of family relationships in ways that can compromise mental health, marital satisfaction, and children's subsequent development (Cowan and Cowan 1995). I agree with Cowan and Cowan that the stakes are high in this transition and that there is plenty of justification for systematically providing support to new parents.

Hospital staff and child birth educators are uniquely situated to address and support parenting as a joint venture, because when a man and a woman become parents together, they tend to attend childbirth classes and the birth of their baby together. Yet pre- and post-natal education are currently underused as opportunities to change dichotomized imagery of mothers and fathers. Instead, they focus on getting babies born and breast-fed, the only two areas in which it is difficult not to conceptualize fathers as just helpers to mothers. I do not mean to suggest that mothers should not be given special support after giving birth and in the process of establishing breast-feeding (if they choose to), but there is no reason, in the long term, to conceptualize men as having any less responsibility, investment, and ability to care for children than women. Childbirth educators have the opportunity and the audience to do much more to relieve stress associated with the transition to parenthood by anticipating the many issues that come up in the care of babies and in the relationship between new parents.

Having said this, mothers tend to have different and more difficult experiences of this transition than their male partners, and it may be useful for clinicians to bring a sociological lens to their struggles. Mothers I spoke with described a loss of autonomy, an overwhelming sense of responsibility, and a sense of doubt about their own behavior that could contribute to anxiety or depression that a clinician might encounter. I want to suggest the value for new mothers of examining social norms connected with motherhood and discussing them with significant others in their lives. Recognizing the pressures and contradictions in institutionalized expectations for mothers may help women to confront idealized images of "good" mothering that they have internalized and replace them with more realistic goals for their parenting. The assumptions that women carry about maternal "instinct," about whether they will replicate their families-of-origin, about how mothers "should" deal with employment, and about what they expect from their male partners could all be useful areas for clinical exploration.

I think it is also important for this kind of analysis not to stay just between a woman and a clinician. This study has demonstrated that mothering does not occur in a vacuum, but is constructed in interactions. For women to express their feelings and thoughts about what is expected of mothers to significant people in their lives may help in the process of developing alternative approaches to institutionalized images. Having a dialogue with their friends, their own parents, coworkers, child care providers, and most of all, their male partners, could allow new mothers the opportunity to let go of negative evaluations of their behavior and feelings.

It is also important that clinicians encourage men and women to work together on these issues and not to collude with the notion (reinforced in academic literature) that mothers are somehow in charge of what happens in the transition to parenthood. Mothers' approaches to mothering emerge in interaction with fathers. Men and women do parenthood together. It would be useful for family therapists to explore the imagery related to good mothering and fathering and to help men and women investigate the ways that their interactions do or do not reinforce pressure they feel as individuals. And until preventive help is routinely available to new parents, it appears that it is worth referring troubled couples to therapeutic services (Cowan and Cowan [1995] report success with clinical interventions aimed at stabilizing and sustaining new parents' satisfaction with their marriages).

Since women are particularly vulnerable to decreases in marital satisfaction following the birth of a first baby, let me revisit some issues that I suspect play a role in this. I think that the lack of acknowledgment of the mental labor that mothers perform, as well as the pressure they feel to be accountable to idealized images, are sources of marital conflict and disappointment. In other words, gender differences in parental consciousness that are not recognized may contribute to the tendency for new mothers not to feel emotionally supported by their husbands.

Women's marital satisfaction may also suffer as a result of their not spending time with other people who are sources of support for them because of the loss of mobility that their sense of exclusive responsibility generates. Women I interviewed who lost contact with social networks became more aware of what they did not get from their husbands in the way of emotional support; they also resented what they perceived as their husbands' greater freedom. If couples shared the sense of responsibility to be available to their baby, neither one would be "free," but perhaps neither one would be unhappy. Coltrane (1996) suggests, in fact, that marital relationships are improved as men become more sensitive parents. And when husbands share supervision of children, both husbands and wives report lower psychological distress (Marshall and Barnett 1995). I suspect that fathers' involvement diffuses competition about who has it worse as well as any envy fathers may feel of attachments between mothers and children.

A recent book by Rhona Mahony (1995: 238, 191) calls on women to "redefine motherhood in their own hearts" and share the care of babies with fathers in the interest of achieving economic equality. She proposes a three-point strategy for women to "train up, marry down in income, and give men lots of solo time with babies." Her rationale is that husbands need an opportunity to catch up with the "head start" that pregnancy gives women and that women must put themselves in a position in which it is not perceived as inevitable that they, rather than their husbands, will leave employment upon becoming parents.

Mahony's interest is in seeing women improve their bargaining position relative to men. My research provides support for the notion that mothering and fathering evolve in interactions and power differences between men and women (as well as in the context of an inequitable social structure generally unacknowledged in social exchange theories). The problem is, however, that mothers and fathers do not necessarily behave and think and feel as they do out of a rational examination of costs and benefits. I would suggest, rather, that parents attempt to ascribe rationality to situations that are, in fact, driven by complex feelings of accountability, anxiety, insecurity, and entitlement. The reproduction of gender is not, ultimately, a rational process.

Mahony argues that if women get themselves into a bargaining position more typical of men—if they make more money than their partners and have no greater attachment to their babies—men will become primary caregivers to children and women will achieve economic equality. But is it really a solution for men to become the harried primary caregivers that women have been? Or for couples to aspire to create gender imbalances in the reverse? Or for "women's work" to continue to be devalued, as women who want equality "train up" into traditionally male fields?

Rather than disempowering fathers per se, what we need is to address gender inequality in the labor market both in its concrete and symbolic forms. Concretely, women should be paid equitably, both in male-dominated fields *and* in jobs that are perceived as "women's work." At the same time, there should be a greater acknowledgment of family and other personal responsibilities in our public social organization. It does not necessarily help parents to be offered extra hours in order to make a decent wage. What they need is to be able to support their families both financially *and* with their presence. They do not need more hours; they need fewer (see Glass and Riley 1997 on responsive workplace policies).

I agree with Mahony that policies directed toward encouraging mothers to leave the labor force just widen the gender gap in who takes responsibility for children. We need policy that recognizes that our relationships to our children and to other people who need us are an ongoing part of our lives that are not finished after a temporary leave. Why not have, for example, a continuous option of hours of leave rather than the single temporary leave of a few weeks? More men might take advantage of this, since it wouldn't entail pulling out of the work force altogether; it would also have fewer consequences for any women who did it (see Schor [1991] for a discussion of employer resistance to this kind of policy). People who are available to babies should not have to bear negative consequences for the rest of their occupational trajectories, and there is still no full explanation for the wage gap between mothers and other women (Waldfogel 1997).

For fathers to take advantage of workplace policies, whatever their form, will require a massive change in norms and images in all of the areas that this book has examined: in the messages that parents get from "experts" about who and what babies need; in social constructions of families and marriages; and in what people see when they turn on the television. It is in everyone's interest, especially children's, to work to change the social construction of fathers as more peripheral to children than mothers are. Fathers' commitment to children should not require harmony between themselves and their children's mothers; it should simply be expected.

At the same time, it is in children's interests for us to take more responsibility as a whole society for their well-being. We need to confront the belief that children cannot be cared for by more than one adult (the mother). This assumption has consequences for the availability and quality of nonparental care; and for babies living in poverty, it has consequences for whether they are cared for adequately at all.

Caring is not something to try to get out of. Many of the parents I spoke with described parenthood as a transformative experience, and as McMahon (1995: 263) suggests in her study of mothers, one that is "potentially redemptive of society." The problem is that caregiving is both a positive experience of human connectedness and, as it has been institutionalized in our culture, an activity of subordinates. It is an activity that emerges not only out of concern, but also out of compulsion (Abel and Nelson 1990).

It would be nice to think that individual women could make things better on their own, as Mahony (1995) suggests, by redefining motherhood for themselves and allowing men to become more active parents. But I believe the case I've made here — that men's and women's transitions into parenthood are constructed, in large part, institutionally and interactionally. As much as the cultural imagery suggests otherwise, mothers are not in charge. I think it will take a concerted collective effort to change the way that children are taken care of; and this will only happen if it is linked to changes in how care itself, and the people doing it, are valued. As McMahon (1995: 277) writes: "Social transformation is the responsibility of everyone—mothers and nonmothers, men and women."

IN THE MEANTIME

There are many ways that men and women who become parents together can ease their transitions, and the first is having a commitment to do so. Ideological commitment to equality overrides biological connection in lesbian parenting, Reimann (1997) argues, and the same can be true of men and women. It does not even take an ideological position, however, to commit to addressing this transition fairly. All it takes is a desire to preserve a partnership, which is worth trying to do for ourselves and our children. If we use what C. Wright Mills (1959: 5) called "the sociological imagination" and see the connections between personal troubles and social issues, it is apparent that the stresses on individuals and marriages wreaked by transitions into parenthood are too widespread to be explained simply by the personality of individuals or their choice of marital partners.

Here are some suggestions for men and women who are interested in resisting the negative consequences of gender differentiation:

1. *Stay on the same team.* Remember that your own "win" is contingent on your partner winning as well. Having a spouse who feels oppressed or depressed (or both) at home picking up the slack might get you to your meeting or your racquetball game, but it does not ultimately protect your relationship or ensure quality care for your child. If you look out for your teammate's well-being, you are looking out for your own, so be conscious of whether your partner's needs are being served by your arrangements.

2. *Support your partner's selfhood and take responsibility for your own.* When babies are born, people often interpret it as a sign that everyone has to attach to the hip that they carry the baby on. But

people have just as much need for autonomy (and maybe more) after a baby is born as they did before. Don't make your spouse feel guilty about taking personal space, and allow yourself to take it as well. Encourage each other's previous activities and friendships; if necessary, schedule downtime for each of you. Own up to your feelings. Don't suggest that it is your partner's "job" to do something when you just don't want to do it yourself.

3. *Pay attention if you feel like you're trying too hard.* Resist the urge to mandate that your family look like a media family. Don't pretend to have fun; try to really have it. This past summer I was at the beach and my children had gone off to buy lemon slushes with my sister. I looked around at the three families sitting near us and in all three, during that moment, a parent was yelling at a child or at another parent about a child. No one seemed to want to get up from their beach chairs (they had my sympathy), but their children weren't buying it, so they were upping the ante. Don't insist that someone go on a vacation they don't want to go on. Don't make yourself go on it. Avoid big productions if smaller projects work better for you; and on the other hand, if you need to take yourselves on the road once in a while, figure out a way to do it, recognize there is work involved, and share it.

4. *Accept that you have a child.* Once you are spending time with your child, on vacation or a snow day or when someone is sick, get into it. This is a good opportunity to say something about my daughter, who is four years old. Both Leah and her older brother, Alex, have taught me a lot about being a good sport. I was telling Leah that I had a story about Alex (who is now seven) in this book, and that I would like to have one about her. She said, "Tell the story about you and me sitting in the chair." Leah had not been feeling well a few days before, and I had to stay home from work with her on a day that I was sorry to miss. After I had scurried around and made a series of cancellation phone calls, we had dozed together in a chair in our living room. This turned out to be a memorable moment for my daughter, and when she remembered it, it turned into a peak moment for me.

5. *Talk about the pressures that you feel as a parent.* But don't do

it in the context of an argument or when you're in a debate about whose turn it is to get up in the middle of the night. If you feel judged, by your partner or anyone else, address it. Say to your mother-in-law or to your child care provider: "I get the sense that you don't approve of what I'm doing" or "This must be different from what you're used to." Chances are the person will take you off the hook, and minimally, you will feel more comfortable having said what you felt.

6. *Savor the pleasures.* They tend to emerge in the most inauspicious of times rather than when we try to plan them. Always return to this basic truth: Whatever anyone says, your child is happy to hang out with you. Hopefully, your partner is too.

7. *Be proactive in your relationship.* Women are often told to convey their appreciation to their partners; men should do the same. Ask your partner on a date. Try to see how hard your partner is trying. And keep a critical eye on your marriage. If only one of you is compromising, if you are feeling less appealing, if nothing seems funny, something is wrong. If you are unhappy, say so, and get some help. Remember, too, that this is a transition. Whatever feels difficult will not always feel that way, if only because our children grow, despite our own trouble doing so.

Women and men *can* try to make fair choices within a less than fair social context. They can monitor how they are doing parenthood — checking not only how their arrangements are serving them and their babies as a unit, but also whether they are all being protected as individuals. Parents need to communicate, to try to understand each other, and everybody needs to take responsibility for thinking about babies. They deserve nothing less.

Notes

Chapter 1

1. Even though new parents describe an ideology of more equal work and family roles than their mothers and fathers had, their actual role arrangements are frequently more unbalanced than they expected, which can lead to conflict in marriages. The notion of "violated expectations" as a factor in decreases in marital satisfaction has been evaluated in a number of studies of postpartum changes in marital relationships, as well as the idea that marriages are more stressed when couples' sex role attitudes are not congruent with the more stereotypical gender patterns that accompany new parenthood (Belsky 1985; Belsky, Lang, and Huston 1986; MacDermid, Huston, and McHale 1990; Ruble et al. 1988).

2. See Parke and Sawin (1976) for a discussion of research that refutes the notion that mothers are more innately competent at caregiving than fathers.

3. Although some sociologists view cultural schemas as a part of social structure (Sewell 1992), I am differentiating cultural from structural patterns in order to speak to the power of dominant beliefs about motherhood and fatherhood as separate from structural arrangements that influence new parents' approaches to parenthood. For example, the structure of the labor market might lead a new mother to approach her employment by attempting to maintain some continuity in order not to lose mobility, benefits, and so forth; however, cultural messages about the importance of maternal presence might lead her to leave her job. It is necessary in my discussion to differentiate cultural motifs from structural arrangements. My thanks to John Brueggemann for passing on Sewell's analysis to me.

4. McMahon (1995) suggests that motherhood is not simply an expression of female identity for women, but rather motherhood produces a gendered sense of self in women. I agree that gender is produced in women's relationships to their children, but having studied mothers in the context of ongoing relationships to fathers, I also think that gender is produced in women's relationships to men in ways that precede how women and men organize themselves as parents, which I discuss further in Chapter 5.

5. Even though the notion that motherhood and fatherhood have been institutionalized and carry particular expectations has shaped much theoretical

writing about parenthood, it has not frequently been examined in empirical studies about men's and women's transitions into parenthood, despite speculation that women's greater difficulty with the transition may have something to do with differences in social expectations. Feldman and Nash (1984: 75) suggest, for example, that there may be "more exacting cultural demands" on new mothers than on fathers, but we have not had much data about the extent to which new mothers and fathers are influenced by social norms.

6. See Glaser and Strauss (1967) on the discovery of grounded theory. For a more thorough discussion of the methodology of my study, see Walzer (1995b).

7. According to Odent (1992), most women who breast-feed do not continue beyond three to six months. As it turns out, however, breast-feeding is an important aspect of some couples' dynamics—even after a year—which I describe in Chapter 4.

8. I highlight these characteristics of the group of parents I interviewed for the following reasons. One is that while psychologists have used couples in longitudinal research about transitions into parenthood, sociological analysis of parenthood has tended to focus on either fathers or mothers alone (LaRossa and LaRossa 1989 is an exception) or on a special category of parents. See LaRossa and Reitzes (1995), LaRossa (1997), and Marsiglio (1993) on the shortcomings of relying on mothers' reports about fathers. Ehrensaft (1990) and Coltrane (1996) have done very interesting research about couples who identify as "sharing" parenting, which I comment on throughout this book; my participants are different in that they don't represent any particular approach to organizing parenting.

9. There is no indication of whether in the case of Cowan and Cowan (1992) this is because these differences appeared to have no effect or because they thought that they could not make interpretations from their sample; race is not discussed in any detail.

Chapter 2

1. I am purposely using the modifier "parental," rather than "maternal" and "paternal," consciousness because I don't think that there is anything fixed about these differences. My data suggest that particular forms of parental consciousness emerge (at least in part) situationally and interactionally, which I will describe in this chapter.

2. LaRossa and LaRossa (1989) describe the movement toward "traditionalization" after the birth of a baby as a change that is not just behavioral, but that involves a shift in parents' world view. According to LaRossa and LaRossa, in the short term, couples may continue to believe in egalitarianism even if their behavior is contradictory. Over time, however, a couple's beliefs will come to reflect their conduct. Although I do not have longitudinal data, I am suggesting that, for some of the parents in my research, there was reciprocity between belief and conduct. That is, belief in particular imagery generated some behavior

while particular parenting conduct generated beliefs about their rationality, or as McMahon (1995) describes, served as a socializing experience.

3. In a follow-up interview with Phil and his wife, he said the same thing about their second child. He didn't remember having expressed these feelings about his first baby, whom he recalled as an "easier" baby.

4. Fathers that I interviewed did not report feeling like bad fathers if they took their minds off their babies; rather, some expressed stress when their babies had to have their attention. Ehrensaft (1983: 52), in her study of parents who share parenting, quotes one of the fathers as saying that he gets "an empty feeling" telling people that he spends most of his time taking care of his son: "I still have enough man-work expectations in me that I feel uncomfortable just saying that." She argues that fathers experience more boundaries between their paid work and parenting than mothers do, resulting in their feeling that they don't have time to worry at their jobs. Many employed mothers, on the other hand, find plenty of time to worry — in part because the issue of balancing work and family is not perceived as an issue for men (McMahon 1995).

5. As Luxton (1980: 101) points out, women are often anxious because babies are "so totally dependent" and considered to be vulnerable to injury and susceptible to disease. See Lamb (1978) and LaRossa and LaRossa (1989) for discussions of how babies' dependency contributes to traditionalization in parental roles.

6. Perhaps ironically, in a newspaper interview about the fifty-year anniversary of Spock's advice book, he was asked about the problems parents face today. His response: "By far the most common problem is the fear parents have that they'll do the wrong thing" (Kaplan 1996: 1B).

7. LaRossa (1997) presents historical evidence that some fathers in the early 1900s took quite an interest in infant feeding, and not in the interest of their own diets.

Chapter 3

1. These images and an ideology of differentiation between male and female roles were captured in the functional dichotomy identified by Talcott Parsons in the 1950s between "male" instrumentality and "female" expressiveness.

2. Hays (1996) found, and I did too, that stay-at-home mothers in our research often generated some income through baby-sitting and similar jobs.

3. Cancian (1985) has suggested that love relationships in our society are associated more with expressivity than with instrumentality, and because women are associated with expressivity, they are perceived as better at loving than men. At the same time, Cancian points out, because our society values instrumentality over expressivity, loving is devalued. The dichotomy of work and love masks the instrumentality involved in love (as well as the love involved in "male" instrumental behavior) and contributes to a devaluation of the people associated with loving: women.

4. Pleck (1987) describes the notion, prevalent from about 1940 through

1965, that fathers should serve as sex role models for their sons. This father involvement, which was to serve as an antidote for "Momism," or the perception that mothers were too powerful, is interpreted by Ehrenreich and English (1978) as an attempt to reinstate a model of dominant manhood in the domestic sphere. Ironically, father involvement is also prescribed in feminist solutions to the gendered division of child care (see Chodorow 1978).

Chapter 4

1. Evidence of attachment is open to various interpretations; see Eyer (1992).

2. As mentioned above, Mahony (1995) also suggests that differences in solo time with a baby fuel differences between mothers and fathers in levels of attachment. Lamb (1981: 478) notes that there is "substantial evidence that infants form attachments to both mothers and fathers at about the same point during the first year of life." He goes on to say that most infants prefer their mothers—probably because the mothers were the primary caretakers.

3. I want to emphasize that I am looking at this issue sociologically. That is, my goal is not to convince readers to feed their babies in any particular way or to discourage parents from getting advice about feeding their babies; rather, it is to point out the social constructions of mothers and fathers that may be embedded in interactional and institutional experiences surrounding the feeding of babies.

4. According to Ratner (La Leche League International 1987), this was a result of advocacy from the La Leche League and of findings about the superior benefits of breast milk for babies' health and for mother-child attachment. During the 1980s, one objective issued by United States Surgeon General C. Everett Koop was to increase the proportion of women breast-feeding their babies at the time of hospital discharge.

5. Women giving birth at the hospital in the geographical area where the parents I interviewed were from were routinely given a brochure from the La Leche League. I am quoting material from a La Leche League guide not because all of the women who breast-fed had consulted it, but because it is a piece of cultural evidence that underscores the point that embedded in advice about feeding are messages about maternal (and paternal) roles.

6. Hays (1996) cites publishing findings that *Parenting* magazine is one of the most popular magazines among young parents, with a circulation of 925,000.

7. Parke (1981), on the other hand, cites research describing how fathers indirectly influence breast-feeding success through their relationships with mothers.

8. See reviews in Fausto-Sterling (1985) and Mahony (1995).

Chapter 5

1. My thanks to Glenna Spitze for sending me this cartoon.

2. See Arendell (1997) for a discussion of gender dynamics surrounding the interviews of men by a woman.

3. Cowan and Cowan also suggest that breast-feeding exclusively may inadvertently contribute to fathers' feeling that their role in caring directly for their babies is peripheral. See my discussion of breast-feeding in Chapter 4.

4. See Chapter 8 for a more thorough description of Mahony's (1995) argument.

5. Their example of this kind of "mutual empathy" is telling, however, involving a couple in which the husband complained of feeling sexually ignored by his wife: "Laurie, who had had a baby three months earlier, had legitimate reason to turn Tom's complaint aside. But she knew it was his way of saying, 'I feel emotionally ignored.' So she decided to put aside her fatigue and do something that would make Tom feel very attended to. A few nights later, when he stepped out of the shower, Tom found a naked Laurie standing in the bathroom waiting for him" (Belsky and Kelly 1994: 30).

It is questionable whether "mutual" empathy is illustrated by one person putting aside her own needs. This image of a tired but nevertheless "naked Laurie . . . waiting" for her husband is grounded in notions of female sexuality as "a form of service to others" (Gagnon and Simon, cited in Schneider and Gould 1987: 141), similar to some of the dynamics that I described in this chapter. If we also heard about how Tom approached Laurie to make this a compelling encounter for her, it would read differently.

Chapter 6

1. Chodorow's theory has been widely criticized—a testimony to its influence. One charge is that there are class, race, and cultural biases in her assumption that mothers are devalued in a gendered division of labor, although as Andersen (1988) points out, this may be a legitimate assumption in discussing the dominant American culture. Chodorow's theory has also been criticized for its psychoanalytic foundation as well as for its lack of attention to structural and biological variables. Chodorow counters that structural and biological arguments explain influences that conspire to *force* mothers into primary caretaking roles, but they do not explain why mothers *want* these roles (Lorber et al., 1981).

2. See Walzer (1995a). The notion that mothers and daughters are uniquely and universally close has been refuted (see O'Connor 1990), and Fischer's (1991) research about mother/daughter relationships reveals the complexity and variation in daughters' identification with their mothers. See also Sholomskas and Axelrod (1986). Blee and Tickamyer (1986) document racial differences in maternal influence on daughters.

3. Marsiglio (1993) points out the difficulty of assessing exactly whether and how media interacts with people's attitudes while at the same time noting the importance of messages carried by media. I agree with both parts of Marsiglio's message: that it is difficult to assert definitive connections, and that trends in media matter.

4. See Risman and Schwartz (1989) for a discussion of individualist versus microstructural approaches to gender.

Chapter 7

1. Joan Acker (1990: 149–151) suggests that the "gender neutrality" of work organizations is, in fact, less than neutral: "'A job,' already contains the gender-based division of labor and the separation between the public and private sphere." Organizations are structured around the notion of an "abstract, bodiless worker, who . . . has no sexuality, no emotions, and does not procreate." Acker argues that women "almost by definition" cannot be "real" workers.

2. For example, Grant et al.'s (1990) study of physicians finds that parenthood significantly reduces women's, but not men's, practice hours.

3. Volling and Belsky (1991) find that fathers who are sole earners participate in child care based on personal choice, while in dual earner families only contextual factors are predictors.

4. See Walzer (1995b) for a review of research literature related to father involvement; see Coltrane (1996) for findings about what makes fathers do more or less family work. To summarize some of Coltrane's findings, husbands share more housework and child care when their wives are employed more hours. Men also do more if their wives earn more of the total household income, especially if they are defined as economic coproviders. Fathers who are employed fewer hours and prioritize family time over rapid career advancement do a greater proportion of housework and child care. And last but not least, more tasks are shared when fathers get involved in infant care.

Chapter 8

1. Although this is interesting, it should not be overinterpreted since my sample is not a representative one. Nevertheless it does provide some support for the presence of interactional constructions of motherhood and fatherhood among the parents that I interviewed.

References

Abel, Emily K., and Margaret K. Nelson. 1990. Circles of Care: An Introductory Essay. In *Circles of Care: Work and Identity in Women's Lives* edited by Emily K. Abel and Margaret K. Nelson. Albany: State University of New York Press.

Acker, Joan. 1990. Hierarchies, Jobs, Bodies: A Theory of Gendered Organizations. *Gender and Society* 4:139–158.

Andersen, Margaret L. 1988. *Thinking About Women,* 2nd ed. New York: Macmillan Publishing Company.

Arendell, Terry. 1986. *Mothers and Divorce.* Berkeley, CA: University of California Press.

————. 1997. Reflections on the Researcher-Researched Relationship: A Woman Interviewing Men. *Qualitative Sociology* 20:341–368.

Behrman, Debra L. 1982. *Family and/or Career Plans of First-Time Mothers.* Ann Arbor, MI: UMI Research Press.

Belsky, Jay. 1985. Exploring Individual Differences in Marital Change Across the Transition to Parenthood: The Role of Violated Expectations. *Journal of Marriage and the Family* (Nov.):1037–1044.

Belsky, Jay, and John Kelly. 1994. *The Transition to Parenthood: How a First Child Changes a Marriage.* New York: Delacorte Press.

Belsky, Jay, Lang, Mary, and Ted L. Huston. 1986. Sex Typing and Division of Labor as Determinants of Marital Change Across the Transition to Parenthood. *Journal of Personality and Social Psychology* 50:517–522.

Belsky, Jay, and Michael Rovine. 1990. Patterns of Marital Change across the Transition to Parenthood: Pregnancy to Three Years Postpartum. *Journal of Marriage and the Family* 52:5–19.

Belsky, Jay, Spanier, Graham B., and Michael Rovine. 1983. Stability and Change in Marriage Across the Transition to Parenthood. *Journal of Marriage and the Family* (Aug.):567–577.

Belsky, Jay, Lang, Mary E., and Michael Rovine. 1985. Stability and Change in Marriage across the Transition to Parenthood: A Second Study. *Journal of Marriage and the Family* (Nov.):855–865.

Belsky, Jay, and Brenda L. Volling. 1987. Mothering, Fathering, and Marital Interaction in the Family Triad During Infancy: Exploring Family System's Processes. In *Men's Transitions to Parenthood*, edited by Phyllis W. Berman and Frank A. Pedersen. Hillsdale, NJ: Lawrence Erlbaum Associates, Inc.

Benson, Leonard. 1968. *Fatherhood A Sociological Perspective*. New York: Random House.

Berger, Peter L., and Thomas Luckmann. 1966. *The Social Construction of Reality*. New York: Anchor Books, Doubleday.

Berman, Phyllis W. and Frank W. Pedersen. 1987. Research on Men's Transitions to Parenthood: An Integrative Discussion. In *Men's Transitions to Parenthood*, edited by Phyllis W. Berman and Frank A. Pedersen. Hillsdale, NJ: Lawrence Erlbaum Associates, Inc.

Bernard, Jessie. 1974. *The Future of Motherhood*. New York: The Dial Press.

———. 1981. The Good-Provider Role: Its Rise and Fall. In *Family in Transition*, 7th ed., edited by Arlene S. Skolnick and Jerome H. Skolnick. New York: HarperCollins Publishers.

Blee, Kathleen M., and Ann R. Tickamyer. 1986. Black-White Differences in Mother-to-Daughter Transmission of Sex-Role Attitudes. *The Sociological Quarterly* 28:205–222.

Blumberg, Rae Lesser, and Marion Tolbert Coleman. 1989. A Theoretical Look at the Gender Balance of Power in the American Couple. *Journal of Family Issues* 10:225–250.

Boyd, Carol J. 1989. Mothers and Daughters: A Discussion of Theory and Research. *Journal of Marriage and the Family* 51:291–301.

Burris, Beverly H. 1991. Employed Mothers: The Impact of Class and Marital Status on the Prioritizing of Family and Work. *Social Science Quarterly* 72:50–66.

Cancian, Francesca. 1985. Gender Politics: Love and Power in the Public and Private Spheres. In *Gender and the Life Course*, edited by Alice S. Rossi. New York: Aldine Publishing Co.

Chira, Susan. 1994. Still Guilty After All These Years: A Bouquet of Advice Books For the Working Mom. *New York Times Book Review*, 8 May.

Chodorow, Nancy. 1978. *The Reproduction of Mothering: Psychoanalysis and the Sociology of Gender*. Berkeley: University of California Press.

Collins, Patricia Hill. 1987. The Meaning of Motherhood in Black Culture and Black Mother/Daughter Relationships. *Sage* 4:3–10.

———. 1991. *Black Feminist Thought: Knowledge, Consciousness, and the Politics of Empowerment*. New York: Routledge.

Coltrane, Scott. 1989. Household Labor and the Routine Production of Gender. *Social Problems* 36:473–490.

———. 1996. *Family Man: Fatherhood, Housework, and Gender Equity*. New York: Oxford University Press.

Coontz, Stephanie. 1992. *The Way We Never Were: American Families and the Nostalgia Trap.* New York: BasicBooks.

Cowan, Carolyn Pape, and Philip A. Cowan. 1987. Men's Involvement in Parenthood: Identifying the Antecedents and Understanding the Barriers. In *Men's Transitions to Parenthood* edited by Phyllis W. Berman and Frank A. Pedersen. Hillsdale, NJ: Lawrence Erlbaum Associates, Inc.

————. 1988a. Who Does What When Partners Become Parents: Implications for Men, Women, and Marriage. *Marriage and Family Review* 12:105–131.

————. 1992. *When Partners Become Parents: The Big Life Change for Couples.* New York: BasicBooks.

————. 1995. Interventions to Ease the Transition to Parenthood: Why They Are Needed and What They Can Do. *Family Relations* 44:412–423.

Cowan, Carolyn Pape, Cowan, Philip A., Heming, Gertrude, Garrett, Ellen, Coysh, William S., Curtis-Boles, Harriet, and Abner J. Boles III. 1985. Transitions to Parenthood His, Hers, and Theirs. *Journal of Family Issues* 6:451–481.

Cowan, Philip A., and Carolyn Pape Cowan. 1988b. Changes in Marriage During the Transition to Parenthood: Must We Blame the Baby? In *The Transition to Parenthood: Current Theory and Research*, edited by Gerald Y. Michaels and Wendy A. Goldberg. New York: Cambridge University Press.

Crohan, Susan E. 1996. Marital Quality and Conflict Across the Transition to Parenthood in African American and White Couples. *Journal of Marriage and the Family* 58:933–944.

Daniels, Arlene Kaplan. 1987. Invisible Work. *Social Problems* 34:403–414.

Deaux, Kay, and Mary E. Kite. 1987. Thinking About Gender. In *Analyzing Gender*, edited by Beth B. Hess and Myra Marx Ferree. Newbury Park: Sage Publications.

Desai, Sonalde, and Linda J. Waite. 1991. Women's Employment During Pregnancy and After the First Birth: Occupational Characteristics and Work Commitment. *American Sociological Review* 56:551–566.

DeVault, Marjorie L. 1988. Doing Housework: Feeding and Family Life. In *Families and Work*, edited by Naomi Gerstel and Harriet Engel Gross. Philadelphia: Temple University Press.

————. 1991. *Feeding the Family: The Social Organization of Caring as Gendered Work.* Chicago: University of Chicago Press.

Dickie, Jane R. 1987. Interrelationships Within the Mother-Father-Infant Triad. In *Men's Transitions to Parenthood*, edited by Phyllis W. Berman and Frank A. Pedersen. Hillsdale, NJ: Lawrence Erlbaum Associates, Inc.

Ehrenreich, Barbara, and Deirdre English. 1978. *For Her Own Good.* Garden City, NY: Anchor Books.

Ehrensaft, Diane. 1983. When Men and Women Mother. In *Mothering: Essays in Feminist Theory*, edited by Joyce Trebilcot. Savage, MD: Rowman & Littlefield Publishers, Inc.

—————. 1990. *Parenting Together: Men and Women Sharing the Care of Their Children*. Urbana: University of Illinois Press.

Eisenberg, Arlene, Murkoff, Heidi E., and Sandee E. Hathaway. 1989. *What To Expect the First Year*. New York: Workman Publishing.

Epstein, Cynthia Fuchs. 1988. *Deceptive Distinctions: Sex, Gender, and the Social Order*. New Haven: Yale University Press.

Estes, Sarah Beth, and Jennifer L. Glass. 1996. Job Changes Following Childbirth: Are Women Trading Compensation for Family-Responsive Work Conditions? *Work and Occupations* 23:405–436.

Eyer, Diane E. 1992. *Mother-Infant Bonding: A Scientific Fiction*. New Haven: Yale University Press.

Fausto-Sterling, Anne. 1985. *Myths of Gender: Biological Theories About Women and Men*. New York: BasicBooks.

Feldman, S. Shirley, and Sharon Churnin Nash. 1984. The Transition from Expectancy to Parenthood: Impact of the Firstborn Child on Men and Women. *Sex Roles* 11:61–77.

Ferree, Myra Marx. 1987. Family and Job for Working-Class Women: Gender and Class Systems as Seen From Below. In *Families and Work*, edited by Naomi Gerstel and Harriet Engel Gross. Philadelphia: Temple University Press.

Fischer, Lucy Rose. 1986. *Linked Lives*. New York: Harper & Row.

—————. 1988. The Influence of Kin on the Transition to Parenthood. *Marriage and Family Review* 18:201–219.

—————. 1991. Between Mothers and Daughters. *Marriage and Family Review* 16:237–247.

Fitz Gibbon, Heather Moir. 1995. The Development of a Feminist Consciousness in Family Day Care Providers. Paper presented at the 90th Annual Meeting of the American Sociological Association, Washington, D.C.

Gerson, Kathleen. 1985. *Hard Choices*. Berkeley: University of California Press.

—————. 1991. Choosing between Privilege and Sharing: Men's Responses to Gender and Family Change. In *Family in Transition*, 8th ed., edited by Arlene S. Skolnick and Jerome H. Skolnick. New York: HarperCollins Publishers.

Giddens, Anthony. 1993. *New Rules of Sociological Method*. Stanford: Stanford University Press.

Glaser, Barney G., and Anselm L. Strauss. 1967. *The Discovery of Grounded Theory*. New York: Aldine de Gruyter.

Glass, Jennifer L., and Sarah Beth Estes. 1997. Parental Employment and Child Care. In *Contemporary Parenting: Challenges and Issues*, edited by Terry Arendell. Thousand Oaks, CA: Sage.

Glass, Jennifer L., and Lisa Riley. 1997. Family Responsive Policies and Employee Retention Following Childbirth. Mimeographed.

Glenn, Evelyn Nakano. 1987. Gender and the Family. In *Analyzing Gender*, edited by Beth B. Hess and Myra Marx Ferree. Beverly Hills: Sage Publications, Inc.

———. 1994. Social Constructions of Mothering: A Thematic Overview. In *Mothering: Ideology, Experience, and Agency*, edited by Evelyn Nakano Glenn, Grace Chang, and Linda Rennie Forcey. New York: Routledge.

Gluck, Jon. 1995. Milk Men? *Parenting* August:24.

Grant, Linda, Simpson, Layne A., Xue Lan Rong, and Holly Peters-Golden. 1990. Gender, Parenthood, and Work Hours of Physicians. *Journal of Marriage and the Family* 52:39–49.

Gray, Ellen B., Lovejoy, Megan C., Piotrkowski, Chaya S., and James T. Bond. 1990. Husband Supportiveness and the Well-Being of Employed Mothers of Infants. *Families in Society: The Journal of Contemporary Human Services* (June):332–341.

Griswold, Robert L. 1993. *Fatherhood in America: A History*. New York: Basic Books.

Guisewite, Cathy. 1995. Cathy. *Albany Times Union*. 2 November.

Harriman, Lynda Cooper. 1983. Personal and Marital Changes Accompanying Parenthood. *Family Relations* 32:387–394.

———. 1985. Marital Adjustment as Related to Personal and Marital Changes Accompanying Parenthood. *Family Relations* 34:233–239.

Hays, Sharon. 1996. *The Cultural Contradictions of Motherhood*. New Haven: Yale University Press.

Hertz, Rosanna. 1986. *More Equal Than Others*. Berkeley: University of California Press.

Hertz, Rosanna, and Faith I. T. Ferguson. 1995. Childcare Choices and Constraints in the United States: Social Class, Race and the Influence of Family Views. *Journal of Comparative Family Studies* xxvii: 249–280.

Hey, Barbara. 1995. Don't Rush Me. *Parenting* December/January:124.

Hochschild, Arlie Russell. 1983. *The Managed Heart: Commercialization of Human Feeling*. Berkeley: University of California Press.

Hochschild, Arlie, with Anne Machung. 1989. *The Second Shift*. New York: Viking Press.

Hock, Ellen, Morgan, Karen Christman, and Michael D. Hock. 1985. Employment Decisions Made By Mothers of Infants. *Psychology of Women Quarterly* 9:383–402.

Huggins, Kathleen, and Linda Ziedrich. 1995. When to Wean? *Parenting*, December/January:117–122.

Johnson, Miriam M. 1988. *Strong Mothers, Weak Wives: The Search for Gender Equality*. Berkeley: University of California Press.

Kalmuss, Debra, Davidson, Andrew, and Linda Cushman. 1992. Parenting Expectations, Experiences, and Adjustment to Parenthood: A Test of the Violated Expectations Framework. *Journal of Marriage and the Family* 54:516–526.

Kaplan, Lisa Faye. 1996. Spock's advice is still what the doctor ordered. *The Saratogian*. 2 December.

Komter, Aafke. 1989. Hidden Power in Marriage. *Gender and Society* 3:187–216.

La Leche League International. 1987. *The Womanly Art of Breastfeeding*, 4th ed. New York: New American Library.

Lamb, Michael E. 1978. Influence of the Child on Marital Quality and Family Interaction During the Prenatal, Perinatal, and Infancy Periods. In *Child Influences on Marital and Family Interaction*, edited by Richard M. Lerner and Graham B. Spanier. New York: Academic Press.

———. 1981. The Development of Father-Infant Relationships. In *The Role of the Father in Child Development*, edited by Michael E. Lamb. New York: John Wiley & Sons.

Lamott, Anne. 1993. *Operating Instructions*. New York: Fawcett Columbine.

LaRossa, Ralph. 1986. *Becoming a Parent*. Beverly Hills: Sage Publications.

———. 1988. Fatherhood and Social Change. *Family Relations* 37:451–457.

———. 1997. *The Modernization of Fatherhood: A Social and Political History*. Chicago: The University of Chicago Press.

LaRossa, Ralph, and Maureen Mulligan LaRossa. 1989. Baby Care: Fathers vs. Mothers. In *Gender in Intimate Relationships: A Microstructural Approach*, edited by Barbara J. Risman and Pepper Schwartz. Belmont, CA: Wadsworth Publishing Company.

LaRossa, Ralph, and Donald C. Reitzes. 1995. Gendered Perceptions of Father Involvement in Early 20th Century America. *Journal of Marriage and the Family* 57:223–229.

Lemert, Charles. 1995. *Sociology After the Crisis*. Boulder, CO: Westview Press, Inc.

Lewis, Suzan. 1991. Motherhood and Employment: The Impact of Social and Organizational Values. In *Motherhood: Meanings, Practices and Ideologies*, edited by Ann Phoenix, Anne Woollett, and Eva Lloyd. Newbury Park, CA: Sage Publications.

Lindberg, Laura Duberstein. 1996. Women's Decisions About Breastfeeding and Maternal Employment. *Journal of Marriage and the Family* 58:239–251.

Lorber, Judith. 1994. *Paradoxes of Gender*. New Haven: Yale University Press.

Lorber, Judith, Coser, Rose Laub, Rossi, Alice S., and Nancy Chodorow. 1981. On *The Reproduction of Mothering*: A Methodological Debate. *Signs* 6:482–514.

Luxton, Meg. 1980. *More Than a Labour of Love: Three Generations of Women's Work in the Home*. Toronto: Women's Press.

MacDermid, Shelley M., Huston, Ted L., and Susan M. McHale. 1990. Changes in Marriage Associated with the Transition to Parenthood: Individual Differences as a Function of Sex-Role Attitudes and Changes in the Division of Household Labor. *Journal of Marriage and the Family* 52: 475–486.

Mahony, Rhona. 1995. *Kidding Ourselves: Breadwinning, Babies, and Bargaining Power.* New York: BasicBooks.

Margolis, Maxine L. 1984. *Mothers and Such.* Berkeley: University of California Press.

Marshall, Harriette. 1991. The Social Construction of Motherhood: An Analysis of Childcare and Parenting Manuals. In *Motherhood: Meanings, Practices and Ideologies*, edited by Ann Phoenix, Anne Woollett, and Eva Lloyd. Newbury Park: Sage Publications.

Marshall, Nancy L. and Rosalind C. Barnett. 1995. Child Care, Division of Labor, and Parental Emotional Well-Being Among Two-Earner Couples. Paper presented at the 90th Annual Meeting of the American Sociological Association, Washington, D.C.

Marsiglio, William. 1993. Contemporary Scholarship on Fatherhood: Culture, Identity, and Conduct. *Journal of Family Issues* 14: 484–509.

Mason, Karen Oppenheim, and Karen Kuhlthau. 1989. Determinants of Child Care Ideals among Mothers of Preschool-Aged Children. *Journal of Marriage and the Family* 51: 593–603.

Mason, Kelly, and Maureen Perry-Jenkins. 1997. He Said, She Said: Divergent Views of Marital Roles Across the Transition to Parenthood. Paper presented at the Annual Conference of the National Council on Family Relations, Arlington, VA.

McHale, Susan M., and Ted L. Huston. 1984. Men and Women as Parents: Sex Role Orientations, Employment, and Parental Roles with Infants. *Child Development* 55: 1349–1361.

McKee, Lorna. 1982. Fathers' Participation in Infant Care: A Critique. In *The Father Figure*, edited by Lorna McKee and Margaret O'Brien. New York: Tavistock Publications.

McKim, Margaret K. 1987. Transition to What? New Parents' Problems in the First Year. *Family Relations* 36: 22–25.

McMahon, Martha. 1995. *Engendering Motherhood: Identity and Self-Transformation in Women's Lives.* New York: The Guilford Press.

Messner, Michael. 1992. Boyhood, Organized Sports, and the Construction of Masculinities. In *Men's Lives*, 2nd ed., edited by Michael S. Kimmel and Michael A. Messner. New York: Macmillan Publishing Company.

Miller, Brent C., and Donna L. Sollie. 1980. Normal Stresses During the Transition to Parenthood. *Family Relations* 29: 459–465.

Mills, C. Wright. 1959. *The Sociological Imagination.* New York: Oxford University Press.

Morgan, Karen Christman, and Ellen Hock. 1984. A Longitudinal Study of Psychosocial Variables Affecting the Career Patterns of Women with Young Children. *Journal of Marriage and the Family* (May): 383–390.

Munch, Allison, McPherson, J. Miller, and Lynn Smith-Lovin. 1997. Gender, Children, and Social Contact: The Effects of Childrearing For Men and Women. *American Sociological Review* 62: 509–520.

Nelson, Margaret K. 1994. Family Day Care Providers: Dilemmas of Daily Practice. In *Mothering: Ideology, Experience, and Agency*, edited by Evelyn Nakano Glenn, Grace Chang, and Linda Rennie Forcey. New York: Routledge.

Nock, Steven L. 1987. The Symbolic Meaning of Childbearing. *Journal of Family Issues* 8: 373–393.

O'Connor, Pat. 1990. The Adult Mother/Daughter Relationship: A Uniquely and Universally Close Relationship? *The Sociological Review* 38: 293–323.

————. 1991. Women's Experience of Power Within Marriage: An Inexplicable Phenomenon? *The Sociological Review* 39: 823–842.

Odent, Michael. 1992. *The Nature of Birth and Breast-feeding*. Westport, CT: Bergin & Garvey.

Osmond, Marie Withers, and Barrie Thorne. 1993. Feminist Theories: The Social Construction of Gender in Families and Society. In *Sourcebook of Family Theories and Methods: A Contextual Approach*, edited by P. G. Boss, W. J. Doherty, R. LaRossa, W. R. Schumm, and S. K. Steinmetz. New York: Plenum Press.

Parke, Ross D. 1981. *Fathers*. Cambridge: Harvard University Press.

Parke, Ross D., and Douglas B. Sawin. 1976. The Father's Role in Infancy: A Reevaluation. *The Family Coordinator* 25: 365–371.

Pleck, Joseph H. 1981. *The Myth of Masculinity*. Cambridge: The MIT Press.

————. 1987. American Fathering in Historical Perspective. In *Changing Men*, edited by Michael S. Kimmel. Newbury Park: Sage Publications.

Rapoport, Rhona, Rapoport, Robert N., and Ziona Strelitz with Stephen Kew. 1977. *Fathers, Mothers and Others*. London: Routledge & Kegan Paul.

Rapp, Gail S., and Sally A. Lloyd. 1989. The Role of "Home as Haven" Ideology in Child Care Use. *Family Relations* 38: 426–430.

Reinharz, Shulamit with the assistance of Lynn Davidman. 1992. *Feminist Methods in Social Research*. New York: Oxford University Press.

Reimann, Renate. 1997. Does Biology Matter?: Lesbian Couples' Transition to Parenthood and Their Division of Labor. *Qualitative Sociology* 20: 153–185.

Reskin, Barbara, and Irene Padavic. 1994. *Women and Men at Work*. Thousand Oaks, CA: Pine Forge Press.

Rich, Adrienne. 1976. *Of Woman Born*. New York: W. W. Norton & Company.

Richards, Martin P. M. 1982. How Should We Approach the Study of Fathers? In *The Father Figure*, edited by Lorna McKee and Margaret O'Brien. New York: Tavistock Publications.

Ridgeway, Cecilia. 1997. Interaction and the Conservation of Gender Inequality: Considering Employment. *American Sociological Review* 62:218–235.

Risman, Barbara J. and Pepper Schwartz. 1989. Being Gendered: A Microstructural View of Intimate Relationships. In *Gender in Intimate Relationships: A Microstructural Approach*, edited by Barbara J. Risman and Pepper Schwartz. Belmont, CA: Wadsworth Publishing Company.

Ritzer, George. 1983, 1988. *Sociological Theory*. New York: Alfred A. Knopf.

Rossi, Alice S. 1968. Transition to Parenthood. *Journal of Marriage and the Family* 30:26–39.

———. 1985. Gender and Parenthood. In *Gender and the Life Course*, edited by Alice S. Rossi. New York: Aldine Publishing Company.

Rothman, Barbara Katz. 1989. *Recreating Motherhood*. New York: W. W. Norton & Company.

Rubiner, Betsy. 1997. Missing data about fathers produce distorted picture of today's families. *The Saratogian*, 2 December.

Ruble, Diane N., Fleming, Alison S., Hackel, Lisa S., and Charles Stangor. 1988. Changes in the Marital Relationship During the Transition to First Time Motherhood: Effects of Violated Expectations Concerning Division of Household Labor. *Journal of Personality and Social Psychology*. 55:78–87.

Ruddick, Sara. 1983. Maternal Thinking. In *Mothering: Essays in Feminist Theory*. Savage, MD: Rowman & Littlefield Publishers, Inc.

Sanchez, Laura, and Elizabeth Thomson. 1997. Becoming Mothers and Fathers: Parenthood, Gender, and the Division of Labor. *Gender & Society* 11:747–772.

Scarr, Sandra. 1990. Mother's Proper Place: Children's Needs and Women's Rights. *Journal of Social Behavior and Personality* 5:507–515.

Scarr, Sandra, Phillips, Deborah, and Kathleen McCartney. 1989. Working Mothers and Their Families. In *Family in Transition*, 8th ed., edited by Arlene S. Skolnick and Jerome H. Skolnick. New York: HarperCollins Publishers, Inc.

Schneider, Beth E., and Meredith Gould. 1987. Female Sexuality: Looking Back Into the Future. In *Analyzing Gender*, edited by Beth B. Hess and Myra Marx Ferree. Newbury Park: Sage Publications.

Schor, Juliet B. 1991. *The Overworked American: The Unexpected Decline of Leisure*. New York: BasicBooks.

Schwartz, Pepper. 1994. *Love Between Equals: How Peer Marriage Really Works*. New York: The Free Press.

Sewell, William H. Jr. 1992. A Theory of Structure: Duality, Agency, and Transformation. *American Journal of Sociology* 98:1–29.

Sholomskas, Diane, and Rosalind Axelrod. 1986. The Influence of Mother-Daughter Relationships on Women's Sense of Self and Current Role Choices. *Psychology of Women Quarterly* 10:171–182.

South, Scott, and Glenna Spitze. 1994. Housework in Marital and Nonmarital Households. *American Sociological Review* 59:327–347.

Spitze, Glenna. 1988. Women's Employment and Family Relations. *Journal of Marriage and the Family* 50:595–618.

Taylor, Verta. 1996. *Rock-a-by Baby: Feminism, Self-Help, and Postpartum Depression.* New York: Routledge.

Thompson, Linda and Alexis J. Walker. 1989. Gender in Families: Women and Men in Marriage, Work, and Parenthood. *Journal of Marriage and the Family* 51:845–871.

Udry, J. Richard. 1994. The Nature of Gender. *Demography* 31:561–573.

U.S.A. Weekend. 1994. Guys & Dolls: Interview with Tim Allen, 18–20 November.

Ventura, Jacqueline N. 1987. The Stresses of Parenthood Reexamined. *Family Relations* 36:26–29.

Volling, Brenda L., and Jay Belsky. 1993. Parent, Infant, and Contextual Characteristics Related to Maternal Employment Decisions in the First Year of Infancy. *Family Relations* 42:4–12.

Volling, Brenda L., and Jay Belsky. 1991. Multiple Determinants of Father Involvement during Infancy in Dual-Earner and Single-Earner Families. *Journal of Marriage and the Family* 53:461–474.

Waite, Linda J., Haggstrom, Gus W., and David E. Kanouse. 1985. Changes in the Employment Activities of New Parents. *American Sociological Review* 50:263–272.

Waldfogel, Jane. 1997. The Effect of Children on Women's Wages. *American Sociological Review* 62:209–217.

Waldron, Holly, and Donald K. Routh. 1981. The Effect of the First Child on the Marital Relationship. *Journal of Marriage and the Family* (Nov.): 785–788.

Walzer, Susan. 1995a. Transitions Into Motherhood: Pregnant Daughters' Responses to Their Mothers. *Families in Society* 76:596–603.

———. 1995b. Gender and Transitions into Parenthood. Ph.D. diss., State University of New York, Albany.

Wenk, Deeann, and Patricia Garrett. 1992. Having a Baby: Some Predictions of Maternal Employment Around Childbirth. *Gender & Society* 6:49–65.

West, Candace, and Sarah Fenstermaker. 1993. Power, Inequality, and the Accomplishment of Gender: An Ethnomethodological View. In *Theory On Gender/Feminism On Theory*, edited by Paula England. New York: Aldine de Gruyter.

West, Candace, and Don H. Zimmerman. 1987. Doing Gender. *Gender and Society* 1:125–151.

Wilkie, Jane Riblett. 1993. Changes in U.S. Men's Attitudes Toward the Family Provider Role, 1972–1989. *Gender and Society* 7:261–279.

Index

families in perpetuation of gender dif-
    ferentiation, 129–130, 133–134
gender as organizing feature of, 2
gender differentiation in employment,
    146–147
"good" mothering concepts, 57
improving power relations, 180–181
individual behavior and, 5, 7–8
institutional contexts, 7
interaction of forces for gender differen-
    tiation, 174–177
mother worry, 35–36
opportunities for systemic change,
    177–183
parental consciousness in, 174
perpetuation of gender differentiation,
    66–67
perpetuation of gender inequality, 14
postpartum care for mothers, 74
social acceptance in motherhood,
    22–23
sociological competence, 13
support systems and marital relations,
    106, 177–178
See also Cultural imagery
Sports, 137

Stress
    from family of origin experiences, 136–
        137, 141
    "good" mother/father beliefs, 46–47
    marital relations, 4–5, 12–13, 103–109,
        173–174, 187 n.1
    maternal, 178
    role conflict, 148–150, 154–155
    social support systems, 106, 177–183
    systemic opportunities for alleviating,
        177–183

Television shows, 139–141, 142
Time management, parent's perceptions,
    23–24

Violated expectations, 187 n.1

What to Expect the First Year, 39–40, 73, 126
    Worrying
    baby worry, 35, 36
    gender differentiation, 33–35, 177,
        189 n.4
    mother worry, 35–36
    parental interaction and, 36–37
    social context, 35–36